TWAYNE'S WORLD AUTHORS SERIES

A Survey of the World's Literature

Sylvia E. Bowman, Indiana University
GENERAL EDITOR

SPAIN

Gerald E. Wade, Vanderbilt University
EDITOR

Gaspar Melchor de Jovellanos

(TWAS 181)

TWAYNE'S WORLD AUTHORS SERIES (TWAS)

The purpose of TWAS is to survey the major writers—novelists, dramatists, historians, poets, philosophers, and critics—of the nations of the world. Among the national literatures covered are those of Australia, Canada, China, Eastern Europe, France, Germany, Greece, India, Italy, Japan, Latin America, New Zealand, Poland, Russia, Scandinavia, Spain, and the African nations, as well as Hebrew, Yiddish, and Latin Classical literatures. This survey is complemented by Twayne's United States Authors Series and English Authors Series.

The intent of each volume in these series is to present a critical-analytical study of the works of the writer; to include biographical and historical material that may be necessary for understanding, appreciation, and critical appraisal of the writer; and to present all material in clear, concise English—but not to vitiate the scholarly content of the work by doing so.

Gaspar Melchor de Jovellanos

By JOHN H. R. POLT

University of California, Berkeley

Twayne Publishers, Inc.   ::   New York

TO MY WIFE

Preface

BY means of this book I should like to acquaint the reader with a man who embodies the best of Enlightenment Spain. His personality is greater than any of his works, but it is only through these works that we can try to approach it. Jovellanos wrote on several broad areas of interest. I have taken up these areas in the roughly chronological order which the author's circumstances imposed on them; and for each, I have tried to provide the reader with a notion of Jovellanos' principal works, supplemented by references to his other writings. I have sought to examine the significance of Jovellanos' thought and writings in themselves and in the historical process, as well as the relations among the different facets of a single mind. In doing so, I have tended to deal, in effect, with the work, and not only the works, of Jovellanos, a tendency which the nature of this author's writings makes, I believe, not only inevitable, but desirable. In keeping with the norms of the Twayne World Authors Series, I have quoted Jovellanos in the original Spanish only when, as in the case of some poems, it seemed to me particularly desirable to make the author's unadulterated style accessible to those readers who may know his language. All other quotations are in translation; and since Jovellanos' works are not available in English, these translations, as well as those of other foreign authors, are mine.

In order to save space in references, most of which are given parenthetically within the text, I have used Roman numerals, followed by Arabic ones, and a letter (e.g., II, 125b) to indicate the volume, page, and, where pertinent, column in Jovellanos' *Obras publicadas e inéditas*, 5 vols., ed. Cándido Nocedal (I and II) and Miguel Artola (III, IV, V), Biblioteca de Autores Españoles, XLVI, L, LXXXV, LXXXVI, LXXXVII (Madrid, 1858-1956). I have not given the title of the particular essay or report thus referred to unless such information is of special interest. A similar combination of numbers, preceded by the letter "D" (e.g., D I, 317), refers to volume and page in Jovellanos' *Diarios*, ed. Julio Somoza, 3 vols. (Oviedo, 1953-1955). Other references and abbreviations are appropriately explained in the notes.

Unfortunately for one who rushes in to undertake a task such as this one, the areas with which Jovellanos concerned himself are vast. Leaving aside poetry, a major subject in itself, they include such fields as economics and political theory, and this at a time when they were undergoing profound changes. Each area, in effect, deserves a book for itself, although then some of the total vision which I hope to convey might be lost. Under these circumstances, this book cannot expect to say much, if anything, new to specialists in Jovellanos and his work. If, however, it succeeds in presenting Jovellanos to the interested and educated layman and is perhaps even of some use to the scholar outside this limited field, it will not be a failure.

J. H. R. P.

Madrid; June, 1970

Contents

Chronology

1744   January 5: Jovellanos is born in Gijón. He is christened on the following day and given the names of the Magi and the Virgin: Baltasar Melchor Gaspar María, though Gaspar was to prevail.

1757   Jovellanos receives the first tonsure and begins his studies at the University of Oviedo.

1759   Jovellanos enters the University of Ávila to study canon law.

1761   June 9: Baccalaureate degree in canon law from the University of Osma.

1763   November 4: Licentiate in canon law, University of Ávila.

1764   May 10: Jovellanos is appointed a student in the Colegio Mayor de San Ildefonso of the University of Alcalá de Henares.

1764   December 24: Baccalaureate degree in canon law from the University of Alcalá de Henares.

1767   Jovellanos decides to compete for a canonry in the Cathedral of Tuy.

1768   February 13: Jovellanos is appointed a criminal magistrate in Seville. He goes to that city.

1768   Approximate date of Jovellanos' earliest known poems.

1769   Jovellanos writes the tragedy *Pelayo.*

1773   Jovellanos writes the prose drama *El delincuente honrado* (*The Honorable Culprit*).

1774   First performance of *The Honorable Culprit.* March 15: Jovellanos is promoted in the magistrature.

1775   Joins the Economic Society of Seville.

1776   July: "Carta de Jovino a sus amigos salmantinos" ("Letter from Jovino [Jovellanos] to his Salamancan Friends"), a verse epistle.

1778   August 27: Jovellanos is appointed a magistrate in Madrid. October 13: Arrives in Madrid. Joins the Economic Society of Madrid.

1779   Jovellanos meets Francisco de Cabarrús. July: First version of the "Epístola de Fabio (*or* Jovino) a Anfriso" ("Epistle from Fabio to Anfriso").

1780   Jovellanos is named to the Academies of History and Fine Arts. August 21: Is relieved of the magistrature and appointed to the Council of Military Orders.

1781   Jovellanos meets Juan Meléndez Valdés after a correspondence of some years. April 22: *Discurso sobre los medios de promover la felicidad de Asturias* (*An Address on the Means of Promoting the Prosperity of Asturias*). July 14: *Elogio de las bellas artes* (*In Praise of the Fine Arts*).

1782   First performance of *Pelayo*. February 20: Jovellanos is named to the Academy of Canon Law.

1782-   Jovellanos writes a series of letters to Antonio Ponz, de-
1792   scribing landscapes, architecture, and customs.

1783   Jovellanos is appointed to the Royal Spanish Academy and to the Royal Commission on Commerce, Currency, and Mines.

1784   March 12: *Discurso sobre el establecimiento de un montepío para los nobles de la Corte* (*An Address on the Establishment of a Welfare Fund for Nobles in the Capital*).

1785   June 19: Jovellanos is appointed to the Academy of Public Law. November 9: *Informe sobre el libre ejercicio de las artes* (*Report on the Free Exercise of Crafts*).

1786   April 6: Jovellanos' First Satire is published in *El Censor.*

1787   May 31: *El Censor* publishes Jovellanos' Second Satire.

1788   January 19: *Elogio de Ventura Rodríguez* (*Eulogy of Ventura Rodríguez*). November 8: *Elogio de Carlos III* (*Eulogy of Charles III*).

1790   August 16: *Reglamento para el Colegio de Calatrava* (*Regulations for the College of Calatrava*). August 28: After trying to intervene on behalf of Cabarrús, Jovellanos is sent to Asturias. December 29: *Memoria para el arreglo de la policía de espectáculos y diversiones públi-*

cas, y sobre su origen en España (*Report on the Regulation of Spectacles and Public Entertainments and on their Origin in Spain*).

1794   January 7: Inauguration of the Royal Asturian Institute. April 26: Jovellanos sends his *Informe en el expediente de ley agraria* (*Report on the Agrarian Law*) to the Economic Society of Madrid.

1795   Publication of the *Report on the Agrarian Law*.

1797   October 16: Jovellanos receives word of his appointment as Ambassador to Russia. November 27: Returns to Madrid as Minister of Justice.

1798   August 15: Is relieved of his ministry and ordered to return to Asturias.

1799   A manuscript translation of Rousseau's *Social Contract* praises Jovellanos in a note.

1800   Anonymous secret accusations against Jovellanos.

1801   March 13: Jovellanos is arrested. April 18: Is confined in the Carthusian monastery of Valldemossa on Majorca.

1802   May 5: Jovellanos is confined in the castle of Bellver, outside Palma. *Tratado teórico-práctico de enseñanza* (*Theoretical-Practical Treatise on Education*).

1802-   Jovellanos prepares several studies on the castle of
1807   Bellver and on Palma.

1808   April 5: By order of Ferdinand VII, dated March 22, 1808, Jovellanos is released from imprisonment. May 20: Arrives in Barcelona. August 16, 1808-August 28, 1811: Correspondence with Lord Holland. September 1808: Jovellanos breaks with Cabarrús over the latter's adherence to Bonaparte. September 25: Begins his work as a member of the Junta Central. December 17: Arrives in Seville with the Junta Central.

1809   November 16: *Bases para la formación de un plan general de instrucción pública* (*Bases for the Formation of a General Plan of Public Education*).

1810   January 27: The Junta Central arrives at the Isla de León, near Cadiz. January 31: Dissolution of the Junta Central. February 26: Jovellanos leaves Cadiz. March 6, 1810-July 17, 1811: Jovellanos stays in Muros (Galicia).

1811   Publication of *Memoria en defense de la Junta Central*

(*Defense of the Junta Central*), written in 1810. August 6 or 7: Jovellanos returns to Gijón. November 6: The French advance obliges Jovellanos to flee from Gijón. November 27: Jovellanos dies of pneumonia in Puerto de Vega (Asturias).

CHAPTER 1

Jovellanos: Life and Times

I *The Dawn of the Enlightenment*

G ASPAR Melchor de Jovellanos was born on January 5,
1744, in Gijón, a seaport of five or six thousand inhabitants, in the Principality of Asturias (now the province of
Oviedo), on the northern coast of Spain. His parents, Francisco
Gregorio de Jovellanos (or Jove Llanos, as the name was also
written) and Francisca Apolinaria Jove Ramírez, came of old
and noble families and raised their numerous children, of whom
Gaspar was the tenth, in an impressive house whose stone
skeleton still stands on the Plaza de Jovellanos, at the edge of
the oldest part of the town.[1]

The reign of Philip V was nearing its end when Jovellanos was
born. Spanning, with a minor interruption, the first forty-six
years of the eighteenth century, it was, especially by contrast
with the stagnation that preceded it, a period of incipient reform and considerable cultural activity. Philip, the first Bourbon
to occupy the Spanish throne, enlarged the role of the state in
cultural and intellectual life, following the example of his grand-
father, Louis XIV of France. On the incentive or with the support of the government in Madrid, learned academies were
founded, the Royal (later National) Library was established, and
protection was given to men of letters. An intellectual pioneer,
Fray Benito Jerónimo Feijóo—Benedictine monk, professor of
theology, and admirer of Bacon—a self-proclaimed "free citizen
of the republic of letters," opened windows onto the new
thought of the rest of Europe through his lucid, amazingly varied, and still fascinating essays. Ignacio de Luzán returned from
years of residence in Italy to publish his *La Poética* (*Poetics*),
1737, the manifesto of Spanish Neoclassicism. Literary theory
ultimately derived from Aristotle thus challenged the Baroque,

now deemed extravagant, at the same time that Feijóo led the attack on scholasticism and Aristotelian philosophy. Reason was the authority invoked by both of these shapers of eighteenth-century Spanish thought: for Luzán, the rules of poetry were drawn by reason from the study of nature and of the great models of antiquity; for Feijóo, reason, or "demonstration," was to guide man in that "hemisphere of the intellectual world" which was not oriented toward revelation and grace. Jovellanos' generation were the heirs of these men.

II *Charles III: Enlightened Despotism*

The work of the Enlightenment continued during the peaceful years of King Ferdinand VI (1746-1759) and culminated in the long and distinguished reign of Charles III (1759-1788). King Charles, the third son of Philip V, succeeded to the crown upon the death without issue of his half-brother Ferdinand; Philip's oldest son, briefly king as Louis I, had died in 1724. Not appearing to be destined for the Spanish throne, Charles had served a long apprenticeship as ruler of Bourbon lands in Italy, first as Duke of Parma (1731-1734), then as King of the Two Sicilies (1734-1759). From Italy he imported his ministers Squillace and Grimaldi, later bringing to power a number of distinguished Spaniards, among whom the most notable were the Count of Aranda, an aristocratic soldier, and two lawyers of good family subsequently ennobled for their services: José Moñino, who became Count of Floridablanca, and Pedro Rodríguez Campomanes, made Count of Campomanes. Under the leadership of these men, and with the concurrence of the king, the government of Charles III came to exemplify for Spain that political ideal called Enlightened Despotism. It was a government which sought sincerely, though perhaps not always successfully, to rule for the benefit of the people; but the very presumption that "the people" needed to be educated and elevated precluded their sharing in power, which was exercised by an elite of birth and, increasingly, of talent under the motto "Everything for the people, but without the people."

The well-intentioned but often arbitrary regime of Charles III brooked no interference with its authority; and its centralizing

tendency brought it into conflict with the strongest autono-
mous or semiautonomous body within its borders, the Roman
Catholic Church. The struggle between Church and State was
fought on three main fronts. One of these involved the Society
of Jesus, long one of the most powerful religious orders in Europe and widely considered subversive because of its loyalty to
the pope and its opposition to monarchy by divine right. The
Jesuits were persecuted throughout Europe; in Spain they were
accused of complicity in the widespread riots of 1766 and subsequently expelled in 1767. Not satisfied with expulsion, the
allied Bourbon monarchs, largely through the efforts of Moñino,
convinced the pope to abolish the Society in 1773.

Another "state within the state" was the Holy Office of Inquisition, which enjoyed a certain autonomy in investigating and
judging questions of faith and morals, claimed special privileges
for its functionaries, and, though no longer very active in persecuting the persons of heretics, was influential in the censorship of publications. The government sought to expand its power
while curtailing that of the Inquisition, a process not completed
until the abolition of the Holy Office in the nineteenth century.

The third front on which Enlightened Despotism moved
against the Church was economic. The pious practice of be-
queathing property, and particularly land, to religious institutions in mortmain, that is, in inalienable possession, had helped
to concentrate land in hands which could only acquire and never dispose. Economists had argued that such concentration discouraged efficient cultivation and economic development, and
the government claimed the right to regulate such acquisitions.

On each of these three major issues, many churchmen sided
with the crown; but others saw only threats to the sacred and
hence inviolable rights of the Church, while the king and his
ministers argued that they sought only to reassert the inviolable
rights of the temporal sovereign without invading their opponents' just spiritual authority.

The government of Charles III concerned itself also with educational reform, establishing a model secondary school in
Madrid and attempting to correct abuses in the universities and
adjust their curricula to modern intellectual trends. These efforts were only partially successful, since many professors, in

Spain as elsewhere in Europe, fought a rearguard action in defense of scholasticism. Economic development was favored through a program of public works, canals, and roads. Establishment of new industries was encouraged, foreign artisans were protected, and technical information was disseminated. Trade was to be aided by the establishment of a national bank, and an ambitious program to populate waste lands with Catholic foreigners was undertaken. In all these fields the government sought to establish its authority and to use it for what it considered the benefit of the people. Economic societies founded by private citizens received the support of the government, which often requested their advice.

In foreign affairs, the reign of Charles III was less felicitous. A perpetual alliance with his French cousins involved the king in repeated wars against the British, including the war which established the independence of the United States; and although Spanish forces were able to recapture the Balearic island of Menorca, seized by Great Britain at the beginning of the century, they failed to do the same for Gibraltar, which even today remains the only alien colony in western Europe.

III   *Jovellanos' Formative Years: Universities and Seville*

Jovellanos received most of his intellectual formation during the reign of Charles III. He had been destined for an ecclesiastical career and received the first tonsure at the age of thirteen. After early studies in Oviedo, he devoted himself to civil and canon law at the University of Ávila and then, in 1764, received a fellowship to continue his training at the University of Alcalá de Henares. In Alcalá he met the soldier, satirist, and poet José de Cadalso, who encouraged his first poetic efforts. In 1767 Jovellanos, now twenty-three, took steps to become a canon in the Cathedral of Tuy; but friends persuaded him to abandon the Church for the law and secured him an appointment as a relatively minor magistrate in Seville. After a trip home the young man entered on his duties in 1768, beginning an extremely important decade in his life.

At this time his friend and biographer, Juan Agustín Ceán Bermúdez, describes him as follows:

He was, then, well proportioned in stature, rather tall than short, elegant of body, erect of head, fair and ruddy, with lively eyes, well-turned arms and legs, feet and hands like a lady's, and a walk naturally firm and decorous, though some thought it affected. His clothes were clean and orderly, he ate and drank in moderation, and he was courteous in his familiar dealings, attracting many persons of both sexes by his agreeable, well-modulated voice and elegant persuasiveness. If he paid special attention to the fair sex, it was to those of distinction, talent, and breeding, never to the foolish or ill behaved. Above all he was generous, liberal, and even prodigal with his limited means; devout without prejudices, frank and simple, a lover of truth, order, and justice; firm in his resolves, but always kind and gentle with the helpless; constant in friendship, grateful to his benefactors, tireless in studies, and unflagging in work. (Pages 12-13)

During the ten years Jovellanos spent in Seville his formal university education was supplemented by an informal but intense contact with the thought of the Enlightenment, which prevailed in the circle of Pablo de Olavide, the civil governor. Olavide, a Peruvian by birth and a man highly esteemed by the French *philosophes*, had been entrusted not only with the government of Seville but also with the supervision of the foreign settlements in the Sierra Morena, one of the more ambitious and controversial of Charles III's economic projects. In addition to these duties, he attempted to reform the University of Seville, stimulated and protected the theater, corresponded with the leading intellectuals of France, and served as a focus and channel for the introduction of foreign books and "advanced" ideas. These activities attracted the unfavorable attention of the inquisitors. Olavide was accused of impiety, corresponding with dangerous persons, reading and possessing forbidden books, owning obscene pictures, and various other offenses; and in 1776 he fell victim to these accusations, losing his position and his freedom in one of the Inquisition's last and most daring (since directed against a relatively high government official) shows of force.

Jovellanos, attending to his duties as a magistrate, worked for reform of criminal procedures, such as the abolition of judicial torture, and for the more equitable and humane execution of justice. He also, however, discovered new fields of study, particularly economics, which he later called the true science of government (I, 314b). He was one of the first members of the

Economic Society of Seville. Since secondary and higher education were conducted in Latin, he naturally knew that language,
as well as French and Italian; and during his years in Seville he
became one of the relatively small number of Spaniards able to
read English. The attention paid to theater in Seville had its effect on Jovellanos, whose two extant plays date from this period. In eighteenth-century Spain law and economics were not
deemed antithetical to poetry; and Jovellanos cultivated the lyric genres of his time, though he was soon to denounce such verse
as frivolous and unworthy. Through a Sevillian friend he established contact with the Salamanca group of poets: Fray Diego
Tadeo González, José Iglesias de la Casa, and various others, including Juan Meléndez Valdés, Spain's finest lyrist of the eighteenth century. Although younger than some of these poets,
Jovellanos soon became their mentor, together with Cadalso. A
good deal of the verse of this period is circumstantial or amorous poetry, and much ink has been spilled trying to identify the
lady or ladies to whom Jovellanos addressed the latter. Jovellanos never married, a fact less unusual in Enlightenment Spain
than in twentieth-century America, yet one which has also given
rise to conjectures about possible religious scruples (Jovellanos
had received minor, though not permanently binding, orders),
possible unhappy love affairs, and so forth. He does seem to
have had one intense and long-standing attachment, beginning in
Seville and definitively ending in Madrid when he was thirty-
five.[2] Thereafter Jovellanos speaks of marriage only to declare
himself unfit for it when he is in his fifties (II, 342a; D II, 125).

IV   *Jovellanos in Madrid*

In 1778, when he was thirty-four, Jovellanos was transferred
from Seville to Madrid, thus beginning a new period in his life
which was to last until 1790. His academic training ended in
1767; his initiation into the world of the Enlightenment occupied the Seville years; now, in the capital, Jovellanos was to join
the ruling elite and work for the implementation of the principles he had absorbed. After a brief time as a criminal magistrate
he was appointed to a council governing Spain's religious-mili-
tary orders and dealing with matters of ecclesiastical, economic,

and educational policy. From Seville he had already corresponded with Campomanes, legal officer of the powerful Council of
Castile, president of the Economic Society of Madrid, and a
leader in the political and intellectual life of the capital. The
protection of Campomanes and his own talents opened for
Jovellanos the doors of the most prestigious organizations. He
became a member of the Economic Society, of the Academy of
History, of the Academy of Fine Arts, and of the Royal Spanish
Academy, to name only the most important. Through Campomanes he came to know Francisco de Cabarrús, a Frenchman by
birth but a naturalized Spaniard, devoted to economic studies
and future founder of Spain's first national bank. In Madrid
Jovellanos first met Meléndez after several years of correspondence; and here he became the friend and patron of the man
who was to be the greatest painter of the age, Francisco de
Goya.

Jovellanos took an active part in the studies of the Economic
Society. In the Consejo de Órdenes, he was concerned with reform of the colleges which the orders maintained in Spanish
universities. He published two brilliant satires in *El Censor*, the
leading Enlightened paper; and as lyric poet and disappointed
lover, he wrote his best-known verses, the "Epistle from Fabio
to Anfriso." A member of important official and semiofficial
bodies, the friend and patron of rising young men in the arts,
the protégé of the powerful Campomanes, and respected for his
varied accomplishments, Jovellanos belonged to the political
and literary "Establishment" of his day. His fall from this position was to be even more rapid than his rise to it.

V   *An Honorable Exile and a New King*

In 1790, Francisco de Cabarrús was imprisoned for alleged
financial wrongdoings. This news reached Jovellanos while he
was visiting one of the colleges whose reform had been entrusted
to him, and he returned to Madrid to intercede for his friend
and to enlist the powerful support of Campomanes. This personage, however, refused to see him, stating that nothing was to
be done and that he felt no vocation for heroism. Jovellanos,
who had not hesitated to declare himself the partisan of Olavide

after the latter had fallen to the inquisitors, was unable to understand or condone this attitude, which ended his esteem for Campomanes. Having returned to Madrid without permission and having failed to accomplish his objectives, Jovellanos was ordered to proceed to Asturias and there to attend to the problems of roads and coal mines. He considered himself cast into an "honorable exile"; and he was in fact removed from the seat of power and allowed to remain in a limbo, neither condemned nor restored to grace, for seven years.

Thus began a new period in Jovellanos' life, and one of the most fruitful. It coincided with profound changes on the broader stage of Spanish history. Charles III had died on December 14, 1788, to be succeeded by his son, who, though in intentions and inclination similar to his father, was not his equal in capacity for work or judgment of men and affairs. The reign of Charles IV was to founder through the unhappy combination of two sets of circumstances. One of these was clearly beyond the king's control. He had not been a year on the throne when the Bastille was stormed in Paris. In 1792 France became a republic; and in spite of Charles's efforts to save his royal cousin, Louis XVI was executed the following year. The scenes of terror and sacrilege, horrifying to most Spaniards and certainly to the Catholic King Charles IV, were eventually succeeded by the consolidation of a new monarchy. Napoleon Bonaparte, moving into the vacuum left by the executioners, became "consul" in 1799 and five years later proclaimed himself "Emperor of the French." These events, which shook the most remote nations of Europe, naturally affected neighboring Spain; but it was her additional misfortune to be guided at so turbulent a time by Manuel Godoy, whom Charles IV elevated to the highest positions of his government, casting aside the seasoned ministers who had served his father. Godoy, who has been subjected to much scandal and censure, was a young officer of good family and education, favored by both king and queen, who had the poor judgment to raise him, at twenty-five, to the first ministry. In the critical year of 1792 Spain was thus governed by a man who, though a soldier, had had no military experience, no diplomatic experience, and little experience of any other useful kind. With a brief interruption Godoy was to maintain his power and the royal favor until 1808. He promoted education and the arts and tried to win the cooperation of men of talent; but he ultimately failed in the task, perhaps impossible for anyone, of coping with events in France. He was unsuccessful in fighting against the French and unsuccessful in fighting with them against the British. In the meantime attention and resources were distracted from necessary domestic efforts, and the danger of subversion from abroad strengthened the hand of censors and of the enemies of the Enlightenment.

During most of this period Jovellanos was excluded from power. Although he had long been absent from his native Gijón, he was deeply attached to it, and the return to it was not unwelcome to him, though the circumstances of it were. Thus we find him disclaiming all interest in returning to Madrid, yet also soliciting a position there or some public mark of a restoration to favor (D I, 441-44, 509-10). All the while he remained intensely active, as we can see in his diary and letters of this time. He attended to the roads of the province, to the nascent coal-mining industry, and to manufactures; and he carried out a longstanding commission entrusted to him by the Economic Society of Madrid by writing one of his best-known works, the *Informe en el expediente de ley agraria* (*Report on the Agrarian Law*). He continued his interest in educational reform and put theory into practice by founding, in 1794, the Royal Asturian Institute of Navigation and Mineralogy, a secondary school designed to aid the economic development of his native province. Partly on his own and partly in fulfillment of various governmental commissions, he traveled extensively over the north of Spain, everywhere studying customs, landscapes, agriculture, architecture, libraries, manuscript collections, and works of art. He found time to encourage theater in Gijón. In fact, he was the economic, cultural, and intellectual leader and arbiter of the town. Jealousies and intrigues developed around him, and he frequently feared he was spied upon.

VI   *From Minister to Prisoner*

Jovellanos had not been very long in Gijón when Cabarrús, the indirect cause of his "exile," was exonerated and freed.

Cabarrús was taken up by Godoy; and he worked to gain the favor of the rising star for his friend Jovellanos. In 1797, apparently without warning, Jovellanos was rehabilitated, first with an appointment as Ambassador to Russia and then, before he had left his home, with the Ministry of Justice. Thus in November, 1797, Jovellanos returned to the center of political life.

Jovellanos' main concerns as minister were reform of the Inquisition, the old problem of ecclesiastical mortmain, and educational reform, including the modernization of curricula and the substitution of Spanish for Latin as the language of instruction.[3] All of these issues aroused considerable resentment and resistance in ecclesiastical quarters. At the same time Jovellanos was considered to belong to the not very accurately named "Jansenist" faction, which, in brief, sought to limit Church wealth and power and to strengthen the bishops at the expense of the pope and the Inquisition. Jovellanos thus had clerical and scholastic enemies, besides having, it seems, soon antagonized the queen and Godoy himself. These forces combined to cause Jovellanos' dismissal from office on August 15, 1798. Whether or not there were, as has long been alleged, efforts at the same time to poison him, it is a fact that his health was shaken by his experiences. He returned to Gijón to take up his interrupted economic and educational projects, but he was not to find the peace for which he now longed. Secret denunciations were made against him, and a secret administrative investigation of his conduct was begun.[4] His position was not improved by a laudatory reference to him in what was considered a subversive book;[5] and there is reason to believe that Godoy, who had recovered from a brief eclipse of power, considered him an enemy to be extirpated, though in his memoirs he denies any complicity in what was to come. Be that as it may, on March 13, 1801, Jovellanos was arrested in his home. His papers were seized; he was held incommunicado and then sent under guard to Barcelona, and thence to the island of Majorca, where at the age of fifty-seven he began to play a new role, that of political prisoner.

Jovellanos spent seven years on Majorca, confined first in the Carthusian monastery of Valldemossa, then in the castle of Bellver just outside Palma. He asked in vain to be formally accused and tried. His friends were also persecuted, and strict or-

ders were issued depriving him of all communication and writing
materials. The degree to which these orders were executed is
open to question; although some insist that Jovellanos was subjected to the full force of oppression, he managed to correspond
with friends and to write extensively. His insatiable intellectual
curiosity at once turned to his new surroundings; and he set
to studying the landscape, architecture, history, language, and
literature of Majorca. He collected books and manuscripts,
wrote a treatise on education, and described the architectural
monuments of Palma for his friend Ceán.

VII   *Jovellanos and the War of Independence*

The storm which was to free Jovellanos and sweep away his
persecutors was, however, already brewing. The government's
policy of patience and vacillation had avoided the wrath of
Bonaparte, but not his contempt. The weak Charles IV, the now
unpopular Godoy, and the jealous and intriguing Ferdinand,
heir to the throne, all committed the folly of seeking Bonaparte's support, eventually making a humiliating pilgrimage to
Bayonne, where royal father and son abdicated the crown in
1808 and handed it to the Corsican. French troops had meanwhile been entering Spain, ostensibly in order to fight a common enemy, Portugal; with or without Spanish consent, they
set about occupying the principal cities. While the court was in
Bayonne, preparing to abdicate, the people of Madrid rose
against the French on May 2, 1808; and although this spark
seemed extinguished in blood, revolt spread rapidly throughout
the peninsula. Joseph Bonaparte, declared King of Spain by his
brother, found his unwilling subjects forming provisional governments to oppose him and allying themselves with the British
and the Portuguese.

Ferdinand had been proclaimed king before the voyage to
Bayonne; and in the brief period before his abdication, his government had freed a number of political prisoners, among them
Jovellanos, who in May, 1808, returned to the mainland. There
he found a very confusing and difficult situation. He had been
named to a *junta* or committee which was to take power if the
junta left by Ferdinand VII proved unable to carry on; now he

received offers and even appointments from the government of Joseph Bonaparte, which was supported by Cabarrús and other friends. He rejected them, first equivocally and then decidedly, breaking all further relations with the man for whom he had been willing to risk disgrace. Instead he became one of the Asturian delegates to the Junta Central, the provisional government fighting against the French. He was thereafter unfalteringly loyal to the national cause, even when at its lowest ebb he was approached in flattering terms by one of the French generals. The invading armies forced the Junta to flee to Seville, and later to Cadiz; but it continued to govern in the name of Ferdinand, who, during the six years that Spaniards fought to "restore" him to the "rightful throne" he had abjectly surrendered in Bayonne, lived in France as a pensioner of Bonaparte, claiming that his highest aim was to marry a "princess" of the "imperial" family.

As a member of the Junta Central, Jovellanos continued to work for educational reform, writing a plan for public education. He was also instrumental in the convocation of the *cortes*, or parliament, which met in Cadiz in 1810 and eventually produced the liberal constitution of 1812. The geographer Isidoro Antillón, a leading liberal in the *cortes*, thus describes Jovellanos in this period:

He was well proportioned in stature, with a kindly face, beautiful and pleasantly expressive eyes, very neat in his dress, table, and lodgings, elegant in his manners, accessible to all who sought him, and affectionate even in the most serious conversations. He had an excellent memory, an uncommonly fluid and opportune way of expressing himself, and a spirit of peace and reconciliation in all things. Plutarch declared that he preferred that history should say that there had never been a Plutarch to that it should be said he had been an evil man. This was always, in public and in private life, the policy of Jovellanos.[6]

After the Junta was replaced by a regency on February 1, 1810, its former members were subjected to unworthy harassment and suspicions, from which Jovellanos sought to clear himself and his colleagues in what may be regarded as his political testament, *Memoria en defensa de la Junta Central* (*Defense of the Junta Central*).

VIII   *The Last Months*

On August 6, 1811, the withdrawal of the French troops en-
abled Jovellanos to return to Gijón, where he immediately began to work for the restoration and repair of the Institute he
had founded, and which had been neglected during his imprisonment and sacked by the French. A hero now even to his compatriots, he was not able to enjoy their esteem for long. In November of the same year a new French advance forced him to
flee once more. He died of pneumonia in Puerto de Vega,
in western Asturias, on November 27, 1811, five weeks before
his sixty-eighth birthday.

Among the vicissitudes of Jovellanos' life certain factors remained constant. His intellectual curiosity, as a glance at any
catalogue of his works will show, remained boundless. His love
of poetry and art, once awakened, never died. Nature, both the
useful and the beautiful, was always his passion. He never questioned the citizen's duty to serve his country. He never lost faith
in the power of education and practical reason, holding always
to the double ideal he had established for the Asturian Institute:
Quid verum, quid utile, "Truth and Utility." In the pages that
follow we shall see these ideas and beliefs as they appear in
Jovellanos' works. All of these respond to the circumstances in
which their author found himself; together, they are the *summa*
of the Enlightened Spain of the late eighteenth century.

CHAPTER 2

Poetry

I *Eighteenth-Century Spanish Poetry*

THE great Spanish authors of the seventeenth century developed a literature which, while often profoundly moral in its content, as in the cases of Quevedo and Calderón, tended toward elaboration, refinement, and daring of form. The poet Góngora had already banished social function from his work and wholly dedicated himself, in his most characteristic manner, to the production of aesthetic magnificence. The followers of these Baroque masters imitated and occasionally exaggerated the salient notes of their models, so that in the Spanish poetry of the late seventeenth and early eighteenth centuries we find, perhaps, a decrease of inventiveness and originality.

The developing Enlightenment, the mentality which was to dominate the latter half of the eighteenth century, saw the Baroque through the prism of its own rationalism. It prized clarity in thought and expression more than it did inventiveness, and it consequently rejected a poetic school that sought uniqueness and originality even at the expense of intelligibility. Along with rationalism, a utilitarian bent characterized the mind of the times. In Jovellanos' writings we find repeated insistence on the need for *useful* studies, *useful* public works, *useful* social classes. Art and literature also had their own usefulness, which was conceived in the terms handed down from the Classical-Renaissance tradition: the purpose of literature is to instruct as well as to give pleasure, and the poet must therefore join the useful to the sweet (*utile dulci*). The Baroque poets, however, did not meet the new age's standards either in terms of rational clarity or in those of usefulness and clear didactic purpose. As so often happens, therefore, the new period reacted against the old. In Spain, this reaction found a champion and a spokesman in Ignacio de Luzán.

Luzán, born in Saragossa in 1702, was educated in Italy and absorbed the Classical and Renaissance traditions in the place where they survived most vigorously; and he did so at a time when nationalistic Italians increasingly affirmed "their" Classical heritage and condemned the Baroque, which, rightly or wrongly, they identified with their Spanish masters. Luzán participated actively in the intellectual life of Italy and obtained a thorough knowledge of Spanish, Italian, Latin, and French literatures. He seems also to have known Greek, English, and German and to have had some familiarity with their literatures as well. The fruit of these interests and studies was a theoretical literary treatise, *La Poética* (*Poetics*), published first in 1737 and again in a posthumous revised edition in 1789.

In this work, Luzán declares that the rules of poetry are the same and invariable for all times and all peoples. Since art, in the Aristotelian view, is the imitation of nature, the rules of art, including those of poetry, are ultimately derived by reason from nature. They are to be found in the critics and theorists of the Classical tradition: Aristotle, Horace, Quintilian, Muratori, etc. Poetry (meaning what today we call literature) must be useful or pleasing or, best of all, both useful and pleasing. Recognizing the usefulness of innocent pleasure and distraction, Luzán avoided a narrowly didactic concept of poetry. In order to achieve its aims, poetry must also possess clarity and verisimilitude, a concept which Luzán interprets broadly enough to allow for a distinction between scientific fact and poetic likeliness.

Luzán contributed to the critical devaluation of such Baroque literature as the Golden Age theater, which often strained his measures of usefulness and verisimilitude, and Góngoresque poetry, which often seemed neither useful nor clear. He also contributed to the appreciation of Renaissance poets of the sixteenth century as yet untainted by the Baroque, like Garcilaso de la Vega and Fray Luis de León. Luzán's book did not pass without contradiction; but it ably expresses a widely-held view which came to dominate Spanish letters in the second half of the eighteenth century, when the overwhelming majority of Spanish writers, or of those who count, are Neoclassicists.

This term should, I think, merely indicate a general adherence to the critical tradition ultimately derived from Aristotle. It

need not imply "dry" rationalism and the exclusion of sentiment. On the contrary, toward the end of the century sentimental and realistic notes, sometimes called "Pre-Romantic," appear
in the same poets, including Jovellanos, who adhere to the
Neoclassic doctrine. Nor should we identify Neoclassicism with
the Enlightenment, Encyclopaedism, and similar terms which
refer to broader intellectual currents contemporary but not
identical with the vogue of Neoclassic aesthetics.

II *Jovellanos and Poetry*

While a student in the University of Alcalá de Henares,
Jovellanos met Cadalso, two years his elder and, by all accounts,
a man of extraordinary charm. "Perhaps spurred on," he later
wrote, "by such a noble example,/ I dared to climb Parnassus/
heedless of bitter experience."[1]

Jovellanos' interest in poetry must have existed before, but
the example of Cadalso may have stimulated him to write poetry himself. This stimulation was soon reinforced by Jovellanos'
milieu in Seville, where he arrived in 1768 and where all the arts
were patronized by the governor, Pablo de Olavide. In this environment, himself young and not insensitive to feminine
charms, Jovellanos found time among his judicial duties to produce a considerable amount of verse, some of which he collected
in 1779 and presented to his brother, Francisco de Paula de
Jovellanos.

According to a letter accompanying this collection (Caso,
Poesías, pp. 89 ff.), lyric, and especially amatory, poetry, is
"unworthy of a serious man"; and as a magistrate Jovellanos
therefore believes that he cannot publish his work, although he
is willing to entrust it to his brother. He also sketches his ideas
on the history of Spanish poetry. In keeping with Neoclassic
orthodoxy as it had developed since Luzán, our author declares
that Spanish poetry flourished in the sixteenth century with the
imitation of Latin and Italian models, undergoing in the seventeenth a corruption of taste from which it was gradually
recovering.

Jovellanos never significantly modified either his view of the general development of Spanish poetry or his reluctance to publish his verses. José Caso González' edition of Jovellanos' poetry, the most complete and careful which we have, contains fifty-two original poems of demonstrated authenticity, four equally authentic translations from English and French authors, seven poems attributed to Jovellanos, and five poetic fragments. Professor Caso further lists ten other poems which can with some certainty be attributed to Jovellanos but whose texts have been lost. The exiguity of this *corpus* is in part due to Jovellanos himself, who, perhaps with some exaggeration, writes that he burned most of the verses of his youth (Caso, *Poesías*, p. 91). Others, if not burned, must have been lost in the numerous wanderings of their author and his friends, several of whom died in exile. Of the poems which have been preserved, very few were published in Jovellanos' lifetime: the "Epístola de Fabio a Anfriso" ("Epistle from Fabio to Anfriso"), in 1781; the "Idilio al sol" ("Idyll to the Sun"), in 1786; two satires, in 1786 and 1787; a satirical sonnet, in 1788; and the "Canto guerrero para los asturianos" ("Asturian Battle Hymn"), in 1811.[2] All of these publications, with the exception of the "Idyll," were anonymous.

The "Battle Hymn," composed in 1810 (IV, 333a), testifies to its author's enduring interest in poetry, which, far from being only the amusement of his youth, was cultivated by him through all the vicissitudes of his life. Let us now examine some of the principal genres and outstanding works in Jovellanos' poetic production.

III   *Erotic or Amatory Verses*

Most of Jovellanos' erotic or amatory poems can be attributed to his Seville years (1768-1778) or the period immediately following. While the genre does seem most appropriate to youth, this chronological distribution may also reflect the differing fortunes of Jovellanos' manuscripts. A good many such poems were included in the manuscript collection Don Gaspar presented to his brother; his attitude toward this type of poetry, however, must have made the preservation of any subsequent writings in this line haphazard.

In this group we can place Jovellanos' sonnets, which show a certain flexibility of form. Along with the more traditional division of the sonnet into eight lines plus six, we find sonnets structurally (though not metrically) divisible into twelve lines plus two and eleven lines plus three. The language of these sonnets tends to be abstract. Their images and tropes are likely to be conventional ("love's arrow"). To be sure, their subject is conventional, often, perhaps, the fruit more of gallantry than of passion; the form likewise is a highly conventional one, demanding, furthermore, a skill in rhyming which Jovellanos disclaimed (II, 315b).

This difficulty undoubtedly diminished in the composition of the idylls, which employ the then very popular seven-syllable verses with assonance in the even-numbered lines. This rhyming of only the vowels brings greater flexibility through a broader range of line endings. The themes of the idylls are largely related to love: the power of love; the beauty of the beloved; envy of the beloved's pet bird; the power of time to increase the beauty of the beloved and the desires of the speaker, but not his hopes; and that favorite of pastoral poetry, the infidelity of a mistress punished by the infidelity of her new lover.

The language of the idylls also tends toward abstraction. The Fourth Idyll (p. 137), for instance, thematically resembles Ode III of Juan Meléndez Valdés' "La paloma de Filis" ("The Dove of Phyllis");[3] but whereas Meléndez apostrophizes a dove, Jovellanos addresses only a much less precise *pajarillo*, or "bird." Jovellanos' adjectives tend to be conventional. Thus we read in the Sixth Idyll (pp. 139-40): "No sale más galana / por las doradas puertas / de Oriente, del anciano / Titón la esposa bella. . ." ("The *fair* bride of old Titon does not with greater splendor cross the *golden* gates of the East. . ."). In the remainder of the same idyll, we find "the soft bed," "the silvery moon," "the snow-white lily," and "Nature's beneficent hand." In Idyll Fifteen (p. 190) these are matched by "the rapid flight of time," "the fleeting years," and "implacable death."

What is true of the language of these poems can also be said of their imagery and tropes. The sensory images are largely conventional ones associated with either love (incense, altar, chains, etc.) or female beauty (roses, carnations, lilies, snow, etc.).

Among the tropes one distinguishes traditional metaphors associated with erotic poetry, such as arrows and vengeance. References to nymphs, gods (particularly Love), goddesses, and personifications such as that of Betis, the Latin name of the Gua-
dalquivir, give the verses a classical flavor. The Idylls seem to
show us a Jovellanos imprisoned by a strict poetic convention in
which he does not feel entirely at ease. In this he differs from
his friend Meléndez, who, by those idiosyncrasies of talent
which nothing can really explain, was ideally suited to this
same type of poetry.   -

Jovellanos' outstanding work in the amatory genre is the elegy "A la ausencia de Marina" ("To the Absence of Marina"),
pp. 106-7, written in the unrhymed hendecasyllables which our
author preferred and which he managed best. The poem begins
with a reminiscence of Garcilaso de la Vega's sixteenth-century
First Eclogue:

> *Corred sin tasa de los ojos míos*
> *¡oh lágrimas amargas!*
> (Flow from my eyes without restraint or pause,
> oh bitter tears!)

It continues with four extended apostrophes, addressed, respectively, to the speaker's tears, to the beloved Marina, to a person-
ified Absence, and again to Marina. It ends rather brusquely,
leading Professor Caso (p. 106) to consider it unfinished; and
this would explain, he conjectures, its remaining unpublished
until 1956, when Professor Georges Demerson edited it in the
Bulletin Hispanique, LVIII, 45.

The most interesting part of this poem is the last, in which
Anselmo, the lover, breaks the conventional Renaissance-
flavored, somewhat abstract rhetorical tone of the earlier verses
and, alternately speaking of himself in the third person and expressing himself directly in the first (an alternation which also
occurs earlier in the poem), introduces nonconventional elements of sometimes striking vividness:

> Ah, if, Marina, in this bitter moment
> borne on the wings of love he could but reach you
> upon the road! If he could cross with you
> La Mancha's arid plain, if he could follow
> your coach's rapid flight! How gladly then

would my hand urge the mules to greater speed,
if I could share the driver's task and place!
Or, in the dress and station of his helper
ceaselessly would I race and move my feet,
though weariness inflict a thousand wounds
upon them! And how gladly then would I
turn my sweat-covered face from time to time
toward you and offer you so sweet a toil!
Ah, with what yearning would I sometimes come,
shrouded in dust and grime, up to your side
and, climbing on the step, ask you to cool
my forehead's burning with your white hand's touch
or with your lips give respite to my labors!

This passage, compared with most of Jovellanos' amatory verses, is rich in sensory images, especially those of touch. Rhetorical repetition ("how gladly then") is common in Jovellanos' epistles. The hyperbolic "thousand wounds" are also a rhetorical element, contrasting with the concrete details that fill the other verses. These belong to the commonplace world: the coach, the mules, the driver and his assistant, the arid plain, the sweat, dust, tiredness, and wounded feet. In spite of the rhetorical "thousand," how great a contrast there is between this sharply delineated vulgar reality and the standardized, slightly vague, idealized world of bucolic poetry, with its meadows, flowers, shade-giving trees, and musical brooks, where pain and sorrow spring only from unrequited love.

The poetic awareness of ordinary life which appears in this elegy, and which is so different from the poetization of ordinary life, reflects the Enlightenment's concern with the lot of the common man. Campomanes, Jovellanos' political and economic mentor upon the latter's arrival in Madrid, was to publish two treatises on the training of the working class, dealing in specific terms with its needs and activities; and Jovellanos himself, in some of his later writings, is interested in the real conditions of life for the farmer and the city worker.

Professor Caso dates the poem which we have been discussing "about 1770." Thus even at the time that Jovellanos was composing rather conventional, somewhat stilted love poetry tending toward abstraction, traditional rhetorical devices, and the usual trappings of classical mythology, he also gave evidence of a descriptive power more fully developed in later poems. These, like our elegy, use blank verse, in which Jovellanos felt most at home and which allowed him most freely to develop his compositions.

IV *Jovellanos and the School of Salamanca*

Most of Jovellanos' love poems do not rise above the efforts of a well-intentioned amateur. Jovellanos himself, as we have seen, did not esteem the genre; and his desire to move away from this type of poetry and to move others away from it dominated his relations with the poetic school of Salamanca.

Jovellanos came into contact with these poets while he still lived in Seville, through the mediation of Fray Miguel Miras, an Augustinian who was in correspondence with his coreligionist in Salamanca, Fray Diego Tadeo González. In order to introduce himself to "Delio" (González), Jovellanos wrote the verse autobiography "Historia de Jovino" ("History of Jovino," his poetic pseudonym), in 1775 or 1776. This composition has, on the whole, little poetic value. Its atmosphere is heavily Classical, with Latinized place names, poetic pseudonyms for all, and the usual population of nymphs, muses, etc. It has, however, both biographical and historical value; and it was the start of a prolonged correspondence in verse and prose between Jovellanos and the leading poets of the Salamancan group, most particularly González and the young Juan Meléndez Valdés.

To González (Delio), Meléndez (Batilo), and Fray Juan Fernández de Rojas (Liseno) Jovellanos addressed his First Epistle, "Carta de Jovino a sus amigos salmantinos" ("Letter from Jovino to his Salamancan Friends"), mid-1776, pp. 117 ff. This composition in 358 blank hendecasyllables, after an introduction occasionally reminiscent of Vergil and Fray Luis de León, relates a dream in which Jovino sees seven horrible naked figures gathering among somber ruins. Their leader, Envy, complains of the fame which the Salamancans enjoy; and the dreadful crew, in order to deprive Delio, Batilo, and Liseno of this fame, prepare to bewitch them into being slaves of love and abandoning all poetic effort. In answer to Jovino's prayer, Apollo sends a light to drive away the evil band; and the dreamer, now awake, asks the Salamancans:

Shall the mysterious message of this dream
be fruitless, friends? And shall forever love
alone be subject matter of our songs?
How many worthy works, alas, do we
rob from the future ages for the sake
of an illusion sweet as it is fleeting,
a fragile glory that in turn robs us
of the high prize a deathless glory gives!
No, friends;
let us, by fate to higher aims led on,
for our poetic zeal such matter choose
as worthily long memory may enshrine.

Jovino then proceeds to suggest this matter: Delio is to devote his poetry to moral philosophy and religion; Batilo is to
cultivate the epic and sing the deeds of Spanish heroes; and
Liseno is to write tragedies, taking his subjects from the Spanish
past. All three should cultivate comedy.

The narration of the dream occupies almost half the verses of
the Epistle. The nocturnal scene among ruins is described with a
Pre-Romantic delight in the horrifying and macabre; but, with
its mythological machinery, it has a Classical antecedent in the
Allecto episode of Book VIII of the *Aeneid.* There are textual
reminiscences of Vergil, notably: *y pues mi voz, a tu mandar
atenta, / renueva en triste canto la memoria / del infando dolor
. . .* ("and since my voice, heedful of your command, / in plain-
tive song refreshes the remembrance / of a sorrow unspeakable . . ."), which imitates *Aeneid*, III, 3: *Infandum, Regina,
iubes renovare dolorem* ("A sorrow unspeakable, Queen, do
you order refreshed").

The value and effect of Jovellanos' suggestions to his friends
have been much discussed. Jovellanos has been accused of trying
to lead the Salamancans from the bucolic and Anacreontic verse
which they successfully cultivated into absurd tasks either
unsuited to their temperaments or inherently unpoetic. Recent
criticism, however, credits Jovellanos with seeing the need for a
new trend in poetry, for a new poetic "mission"; and it points
out that the directions which Jovellanos suggested were neither
absurd nor contrary to the tastes of his times.[4] Whatever we
may think of Meléndez' aptness for the epic, he wished, quite
independently of Jovellanos, to cultivate this genre; and he was

working on a translation of Homer when Jovino wrote his First Epistle. Delio (González), a monk in his mid-forties, might not unreasonably be asked to forsake erotic poetry for philosophy and religion. In effect, Jovellanos, as a good Neoclassicist, sought a more useful poetry in the service of Enlightened ideals. As for Jovellanos' suggestion that national subjects be used in epic and tragedy, it is no revolutionary harbinger of Romanticism; Spanish Neoclassicism, unlike the French of the "Grand Siècle," never abandoned native historical and literary tradition. Nicolás Fernández de Moratín, Cadalso, and Jovellanos himself, among others, had already written tragedies based on medieval Spanish history; and in 1778 the Royal Spanish Academy set Cortés' destruction of his ships as the subject for a competition in epic poetry.

Whatever the merits of Jovellanos' advice, its effects were real and lasting, and the Salamancans maintained a steady correspondence with him. The published letters of Meléndez show Batilo's veneration for the friend he had never met and who was not much his elder, and his willingness—indeed, eagerness—to submit his work to the guidance and correction of Jovino.[5] Although Batilo never did become an epic poet, his initiation into the philosophical and nature poetry of Pre-Romantic Europe was due to Jovellanos; and on his production in this genre rests much of his influence on subsequent poetic generations.[6] Jovellanos, furthermore, not only indicated poetic directions to his friends but also, through his "correction" (we should say "editing") of their works, exercised a technical influence on their verses (Caso, *Poesías*, pp. 36-37).

Jovellanos in turn submitted his poetry to the editorial discretion of the Salamancans; one of his best, and best known, poems, the Second Satire, was revised by Meléndez. The influence on Jovellanos, however, was entirely technical, not theoretical; and it is difficult to evaluate.[7]

V   *Satires*

Although possessed of high moral standards and a quick and severe critical spirit, Jovellanos was little suited by temperament to the role of public accuser and was often unhappy with his judicial duties. He felt some distaste for satire; yet, in spite of his very limited production in this genre, half of the poems he published in his lifetime belong to it, and his poetic reputation depends heavily on these works.

The satire was a genre especially in keeping with the pre-eminently critical spirit of the Enlightenment. Not only could it judge old institutions; it also examined emerging ways of life, which, as always, seemed to portend a dreadful decline of morality and the eventual collapse of the social order. Furthermore, an age which valued *useful* poetry, which thought that literature should instruct as well as entertain, could not but cherish the satire as the embodiment of these twin aims. Jovellanos' contribution to the genre consists of six moderately witty epigrams and several literary and social satires.

During the time of his residence in Madrid, Jovellanos was involved in some of the literary polemics, often degenerating to the level of backyard squabbles, which abounded in the 1780's. From the middle of these years date the two *romances*, or octosyllabic ballads, "Against Huerta." Vincente García de la Huerta, poet, dramatist, and critic of marked and somewhat eccentric tastes, was himself a vigorous polemicist. His *Raquel* (1778) is probably the best Spanish Neoclassic tragedy, and this success, as well as his theoretical and orthographic peculiarities, were not easily forgiven by his contemporaries. Huerta undertook the defense of the Golden Age theater, which did not endear him to those who sought a total reform of the stage. Jovellanos' *romances,* in burlesque chivalric style, narrate the battle between Huerta and Juan Pablo Forner, with passing jabs at other contemporary literary figures. These compositions, though occasionally witty, are, in their pettiness and insulting tone, unworthy of Jovellanos, who nevertheless took enough pride in them to make him resent Forner's claim to the authorship of one. The same style prevails in a *jácara*, or burlesque composition in short verses, against the same Huerta and in an unfinished *romance* against Forner.

The two satires published in the periodical *El Censor* in 1786 and 1787, respectively, are addressed to a certain Arnesto, who is probably a fictional personage serving only as the satirist's interlocutor and confidant (Caso, *Poesías*, p. 474, n. 212). Both poems are written in Jovellanos' favorite meter, the blank hendecasyllable. The First Satire consists of 167 verses; the Second, of 285.

The First Satire begins with fourteen lines of introductory material, ending with the traditional claim to be attacking the sin or vice, not the sinner. The evil which Jovellanos then chastises is the corruption of women, especially of noble women. He embodies his main theme, adultery, in a figure and scene of graphic crudeness:

> *Hubo un tiempo en que andaba la modestia*
> *dorando los delitos; hubo un tiempo*
> *en que el recato tímido cubría*
> *la fealdad del vicio; pero huyóse*
> *el pudor a vivir en las cabañas.*
> *Con él huyeron los dichosos días,*
> *que ya no volverán; huyó aquel siglo*
> *en que aun las necias burlas de un marido*
> *las Bascuñanas crédulas tragaban;*
> *mas hoy Alcinda desayuna al suyo*
> *con ruedas de molino; triunfa, gasta,*
> *pasa saltando las eternas noches*
> *del crudo enero, y cuando el sol tardío*
> *rompe el oriente, admírala golpeando,*
> *cual si fuese una extraña, al propio quicio.*
> *Entra barriendo con la undosa falda*
> *la alfombra; aquí y allí cintas y plumas*
> *del enorme tocado siembra, y sigue*
> *con débil paso soñolienta y mustia,*
> *yendo aún Fabio de su mano asido,*
> *hasta la alcoba, donde a pierna suelta*
> *ronca el cornudo y sueña que es dichoso.*
> *Ni el sudor frío, ni el hedor, ni el rancio*
> *eructo le perturban. A su hora*
> *despierta el necio; silencioso deja*
> *la profanada holanda, y guarda atento*
> *a su asesina el sueño mal seguro.*
> *¡Cuántas, oh Alcinda, a la coyunda uncidas,*
> *tu suerte envidian! Cuántas de Himeneo*
> *buscan el yugo para lograr tu suerte,*
> *y sin que invoquen la razón, ni pese*
> *su corazón los méritos del novio,*
> *el sí pronuncian y la mano alargan*
> *al primero que llega!* (Pp. 236-37)

(There was a time once when a sense of shame
gilded their crimes and covered timidly
the ugliness of vice; but modesty

has fled the Court to live in peasants' huts.
And with it fled the happy days gone by,
the age when wives revered their husbands' word.
Today Alcinda asks her mate to swallow
millstones for breakfast; and in social triumphs
and dancing spends his fortune and the nights
of bitter January, till the sun
sluggishly rising, is amazed to see
how, stranger-like, at her own door she knocks.
She enters, sweeping with her flowing skirt
the rug and leaving scattered here and there
the plumes and ribbons of her giant headdress.
Drowsy and languid, but with Fabio still
holding her hand, she weakly finds her way
to the bedchamber where the snoring cuckold
sleeps like a log and dreams he's fortunate.
Neither cold sweat, nor stench, nor rancid belch
bother the fool until his time to rise,
when quietly he leaves dishonored sheets,
not to disturb his foe's uneasy sleep.
    How many, Alcinda, are those in wedlock yoked
envious of your fate! How many those
who week that yoke for such a fate as yours,
and without heeding reason and without
weighing their suitors' merits in their hearts,
pronounce their "Yes" and offer forth their hand
to the first comer!)

On the last two lines Goya based the second etching in his series of *Caprichos.*

The passage quoted illustrates the First Satire's alternation between general considerations, expressed in abstract, meta-phorical, and allegorical language ("modesty / gilded their crimes," "in wedlock yoked"), and specific examples, using concrete terms and vulgar, sometimes shocking, details in sharp sensory images like "sweeping with her flowing skirt / the rug" and "Neither cold sweat, nor stench, nor rancid belch."

Attacks on adultery are, in all likelihood, approximately co-eval with the institution of marriage. They were, however, par-ticularly common in Jovellanos' time, which by all accounts, experienced a relaxation of sexual mores, especially in the upper classes and most particularly for women, men never having suf-fered very severe restrictions anyhow. This moral emancipation was accompanied by the rise of a peculiar institution, the *corte-jo*, the "official" and recognized male friend of a married woman. In many cases this relationship was no doubt more or less innocent; yet it must have been essentially unstable, slipping easily into tacitly accepted adultery. Both the *cortejo* and the excessive freedom of the noble woman are depicted in Jovellanos' satire, where Alcinda not only leaves her house at night, but returns to it in the company of Fabio, the gallant who escorts her right into the conjugal bedroom.

While the rich and noble adulteress triumphs unpunished, the machinery of justice cruelly chastises

> the unhappy victims who are dragged to vice
> by poverty and lack of all protection,
> the helpless orphan harried without cease
> by gold and hunger, or who yields to love
> and is seduced by tender flattery.

Jovellanos' strict morality makes him demand equal treatment for all social classes. He sees the individual crime as a result of social as well as individual factors, and so the prostitute becomes for him an "unhappy victim" of society, not idealized in the Romantic fashion but neither, as she has traditionally been, only an object of utility, derision, and scorn. This facet of Jovellanos' attack on adultery reflects the new sensibility and social consciousness of the Enlightenment and the trend toward more humane treatment of all kinds of criminals.

After describing the behavior of Alcinda, Jovellanos proceeds to suggest, like Cadalso and other satirists of the latter eighteenth century, that general frivolity and the spread of luxury are the corrupters of morality. He then matches Alcinda with another concrete but much less developed example, that of "the reckless maiden" whose foolish vanity leads her along the road to perdition. The poem ends with some thirty verses decrying what their author sees as general corruption, frivolity, and venality.

The alternation of the general and the specific, observed in the First Satire, characterizes several of Jovellanos' best compositions. His age strove for universality; and it therefore needed to transcend the particular, and especially, as we shall see in another famous poem of our author's, the subjective. At the

same time, however, the doors of literature were being opened
to the details of ordinary life, necessarily specific and sometimes
expressed with brutal realism. We have already seen this feature
in the elegy "To the Absence of Marina." The same novelty of
language—crude details, "vulgar" expressions—is largely responsible for the forcefulness, the "shock value" of the First Satire.

Shortly after the appearance of this satire in *El Censor,* the
same paper published two letters signed with the pseudonym
"El Conde de las Claras" ("The Count of Plain Words"), which
a distinguished scholar ascribes (unnecessarily, I believe) to
Jovellanos himself.[8] These letters begin by complaining that the
First Satire is not sufficiently specific. According to the
"Count," Jovellanos' poem uses too much allegorical and mythological language and too elevated a style. Furthermore, it is
not harsh enough. The critic believes that in order to do any
good, satire must attack the class that sets the moral tone of
society, the nobility. This class, however, is vulnerable only in
its pride of descent and of wealth; and satire must therefore
show it that its conduct endangers its claim to both riches and
noble descent and makes it inferior to any ordinary but honest
man.

This advice is followed in Jovellanos' Second Satire, published
in *El Censor* in 1787, after the appearance of the "Count's" letters, and usually titled, though not by Jovellanos himself, "On
the Faulty Education of the Nobility." The Second Satire, longer than the First, dispenses with any introductory passage and
immediately presents a degenerate noble who affects the vulgar
elegance and bully valor of that lower-class type known as the
majo. He leans against a corner, wrapped in a huge cape, pale,
dirty, tobacco-stained, with long sideburns and a generally
"tough" air. Although of illustrious descent, he has been
brought up by ignorant and corrupt servants and is himself
ignorant of everything except gambling, bulls, actresses, and
prostitutes.

Almost two hundred verses are devoted to this young noble,
and then some fifty to another type, "a pretty, perfumed, sugar-
pastry fop, / whose noble dress is cover to vile thoughts." Educated in France, he speaks neither French nor Spanish but an
unintelligible hodgepodge of the two. A single verse epitomizes
his life: *Puteó, jugó, perdió salud y bienes* ("He whored and

played and lost his health and goods"). If he does not die young as a result of these excesses, he grows old in "cynical and infamous bachelorhood"; or perhaps he marries and makes a victim of his wife, for vice has weakened him and venereal diseases have "infected the seed of life." This second noble type, less extensively and precisely described than the first, loses individuality as his life dissolves into three possible trajectories.

The Second Satire concludes with a judgment on the class which the two young nobles typify and which Jovellanos compares with the heroes of the Middle Ages and of the conquest of America:

> Where now is Villandrando's sturdy arm,
> Argüello's or Paredes' robust shoulders?
> The heavy helmet, the high plumèd crest—
> were they for sickly skulls, and feeble, forged?
> Who now can wear the hard and sparkling breastplate
> o'er leather jacket and a coat of mail?
> Who now can couch the weighty lance? Who now. . .?
> Return, oh Berber fierce, return, once more
> to overrun the land from South to North,
> for no Pelayos or Alfonsos now
> will offer you resistance; pygmies weak
> await you, and submissive they will fall
> at the first hint of curved scimitar. . .
> And this, Arnesto, is a noble? This,
> the sum and substance of a proud descent?
> And of what use are class and noble race
> if virtue's lacking? What has now become
> of venerated names of ages past,
> of Laras, Tellos, Haros, and Girones?
> What evil spirit tarnishes the fame
> of all their triumphs? Are they sons of theirs,
> those to whom now the throne looks for defense?
> Are these the nobles of Castile? Is this
> the arm, once feared, in which our people saw
> its freedom's guaranty? Oh shame! Oh age!
> The law's support has failed; all falls; the slime
> ferments and haughty spirits breeds who rise
> to the Olympian thrones. And what of that?
> Let common men burst boldly forth and seize
> honors and titles, splendor, noble rank.
> Let all in infamous confusion sink,
> and do away with classes and estates.
> Virtue alone can be their guard and shield;
> without her, let all end and come to nought. (Pp. 252-53)

The Second Satire is less given to general considerations than the First. In keeping with the recommendations of the "Conde de las Claras," it concentrates on specific and concrete portrayals of the two noble types, for whom critics have proposed a number of real models (Caso, *Poesías*, pp. 476-78). In their concrete passages, however, the two Satires are equally vigorous.

As Professor Caso points out, the theme of the bad education of the nobility, quite apart from possible literary models in previous periods, was a common one in Jovellanos' time. To go no further, the seventh of Cadalso's *Cartas marruecas* (*Moroccan Letters*) presents an idle young gentleman reminiscent in many ways of Jovellanos' nobles. *Il Giorno*, Giuseppe Parini's great eighteenth-century satirical poem, treats the same subject, with some coincidences of motifs and wording.[9]

The concept of nobility underlying both Satires is the same that is found in Jovellanos' political and pedagogical writings: the privileges of the noble class must be justified by corresponding obligations, which in the past were chiefly military, but now must be largely cultural and moral. The last nine verses (eleven in the original) of the Second Satire were not published in Jovellanos' lifetime; their message, which foretells the fate of hereditary aristocracy after 1789, is, however, clearly though less strongly repeated in 1794, when Jovellanos warns the nobles of his province that only patriotism and virtue can justify their privileges (I, 323a).

The First and Second Satires suffice to give Jovellanos a distinguished place among eighteenth-century poets by the clarity of their organization, the rhythmic flexibility of their lines, the brilliance of some of their sketches, the vigor of their expression, and the often revolutionary pungency of their language. Satire, however, is only a small part of Jovellanos' work and corresponds largely to the Madrid period of his life. We now know of only two satires written after 1788. Both use hendecasyllabic tercets, favored for this genre since the Renaissance. One is directed against lawyers, in 240 verses; the other is a fifteen-line fragment of a literary satire.

VI   *Epistles*

The blank hendecasyllable, which Jovellanos used to good effect in his first two satires, is also the meter of all but one of his epistles. It is ideally suited to the familiar style demanded by this poetic genre, which, in spite of a distinguished history going back to Classical times, is today practically lost.

We have ten epistles by Jovellanos. The first, addressed to his Salamancan friends, has already been discussed. The second is directed to Jean-François-Ange d'Eymar, abbé de Walchrétien, translator into French of Jovellanos' play *El delincuente honrado* (*The Honorable Culprit*). In rather generalized language, it describes an imaginary visit to the official Madrid of the late 1770's. Its personifications and Classical elements remind us of the allegorical and emblematic graphic art of the period.

Far more interesting is the Third Epistle, "Epístola heroica de Jovino a sus amigos de Sevilla" ("Heroic Epistle from Jovino to his Friends in Seville"), which expresses Jovellanos' sentiments as he goes from Seville to his new position in Madrid in 1778. It is notable for its realistic reproduction of the sensations of the voyage:

> Obedient to the whims of cruel fate
> my body's dragged away, while in a gulf
> profound of troubled thought my spirit's plunged.
> How fast the rapid mules carry me off,
> delightful Betis, from your pleasant shore!
> In ceaseless trot they follow on the voice
> of heartless driver, whom my bitter tears
> move less than them. They follow on his voice;
> while tiresome jangling of discordant bells,
> the whip's harsh crack, the hoarse and threatening cry
> of cursing muleteer, and the wheels' bustle
> as on the steep and stony road they turn
> the screeching axle—all of these combined
> shatter my ear and heart at the same time.
> From town to town, from inn to inn they drag
> my aching members, as if all of me
> already were a corpse, rigid, unfeeling. (P. 149)

The details of coach travel are strongly reminiscent of the elegy "To the Absence of Marina." In the same realistic vein, the traveler's eyes "see everywhere only an arid desert," partly because he projects his sorrow onto the world around him (a projection characteristic of Romanticism, but as old as the eclogues of Garcilaso de la Vega and, indeed, of Vergil), and partly because as he travels northward this is what he actually sees.

Jovellanos' interest in vulgar details was condemned by some critics as unpoetic (Caso, *Poesías*, pp. 457-59, nn. 111 and 116), yet it is both an expression of the interests of his time and a forerunner of subsequent aesthetic tendencies. The eighteenth century awoke to the existence of the popular. Statesmen and reformers concerned themselves with the economic, intellectual, and moral development of the peasant and the laborer; and, on the more trivial yet no less revealing side, the nobles of Spain aped the dress and manners of the lower-class *majos*. Romanticism, in the coming century, was to develop further this interest in "the people" and the popular, along with the picturesque detail. Romanticism was also to proclaim the aesthetic value of the ugly, justifying the kind of ordinary and even unpleasant features that we find in Jovellanos' lines. Unlike many Romantics, however, Jovellanos does not sentimentalize or idealize the popular element. His driver and muleteer are unfeeling brutes, little better than the animals in their charge; they do not resemble the innately virtuous worker and peasant dear to nineteenth-century Romantics and their twentieth-century spiritual descendants.

Sentimentality in Jovellanos' poem is largely subjective. The speaker presents himself as a victim of a "cruel fate"; he refers to his "bitter tears"; and he gives us an apology of that characteristically eighteenth-century delight, sentimental weeping:

> Since when is natural tenderness a crime?
> Could e'en the boldest eye condemn the tears
> shed in the bosom of a spotless friendship?
> Let those men hide their tears who to the world
> give through them witness of their weaknesses;
> howe'er, the gentle heart, open alone
> to the chaste flame of friendship, shall it be
> ashamed of virtuous tenderness?

The motifs of friendship and of virtue are favorites in the sentimental poetry of the latter part of the century; and the apology of tears is likewise to be found in Jovellanos' drama (I, 83a). Indeed, tears, with or without apology, flow copiously, and often not only figuratively, in the life and literature of the second half of the eighteenth century, from Samuel Richardson on. An increasingly morbid sentimentality, quite uncalled-for by the author's transfer to Madrid, marks the closing lines of the present epistle, in which Jovellanos anticipates the coming of old age and of "slow-stepping, lazy death, the only harbor / that offers shelter from life's final ills." "Ah, when," he asks, "will the day so longed for come / to put an end to ever-flowing tears?"

In addition to these realistic and sentimental elements, one finds in the poem literary reminiscences from the Neoclassic tradition. There are echoes of Horace and of Garcilaso, and there is a "literarization" of the landscape which contrasts with the sharply delineated details smacking of direct observation. So depressed is the poet that, according to him, nothing pleases him:

> Neither the joyous fields, richly adorned
> with autumn's gold, nor rustic merriment
> which innocently echoes in the vales
> as boisterous youth steals Father Bacchus' gifts,
> nor the green slopes, where tender bleating lambs
> play with their mothers' overflowing teats,
> nor tuneful birds that warble in the wind,
> nor murmuring brook that winds its silvery way...

Here the pattern of bucolic poetry is imposed on nature. The nature shown by these lines has been observed in books, not necessarily in reality. In other instances the poet observes through a Classical prism, as when he refers to the olive as "Minerva's sacred tree."

Professor Caso argues convincingly that Jovellanos began his poem on the road, and that this immediacy of experience is reflected in the realistic descriptions of landscapes and sensations; but that once in Madrid, he proceeded to "polish" his work and "raise" its tone by interpolating elements which derive from literary tradition, not only from personal experience (*Poesías*, pp. 28 ff., 148).

We find the same tendency to elaborate the immediate expression of subjective experience in order to generalize it or fit it into a literary pattern in one of Jovellanos' most famous poems and one of the few published in his lifetime, the "Epístola de Fabio a Anfriso," or "Epístola del Paular" (in Professor

Caso's edition, "Epístola de Jovino a Anfriso, escrita desde el
Paular," ["Epistle from Jovino to Anfriso, Written from El
Paular"]). This work exists in two versions. One dates from
1779 but remained unknown until it was published by José
Caso González in 1960.[10] The other was probably written in
1780 and was published by Antonio Ponz in his *Viaje de España
(Spanish Journey)* in 1781.

The earlier version consists of 191 blank hendecasyllables
addressed by Jovino to Anfriso, the poetic name of Jovellanos'
friend and colleague in the magistrature, Mariano Colón. After
the salutation, Jovino expresses his desire for a peaceful life of
retirement, inspired by the place in which he writes and to
which he had been sent on official business, the monastery of El
Paular, in the Sierra de Guadarrama, not far from Madrid. This
desire is, however, frustrated by the memory of Jovino's treach-
erous mistress, Enarda, a pseudonym which appears several
times in Jovellanos' poetry and whose bearer no one has satis-
factorily identified. Jovino proceeds to describe the lovely natural setting of the monastery: a river, trees, shade—a *locus amoe-
nus* in the best literary tradition, but this time directly and
quite accurately observed in nature. Jovino, however, avoids
this pleasant place and seeks another setting more in keeping
with his mood: dark, silent, and autumnal (although the poem
was written, or at least begun, in summer). He then tells the
story of Enarda's betrayal. His solitude awakens fear in him—indeed, terror—as well as sadness and a general lassitude, a
taedium vitae.

Fundamental to the structure of the poem is the clash
between Jovino's longing for peace and the irrepressible remembrance of his frustrated love. This emotional contrast is reflected
in the variation between two types of nature: the gentle, recep-
tive, benevolent nature of the pleasance, none the less authentic
for conforming to a literary tradition; and the lugubrious, highly
subjectivized nature to which Jovino flees to ruminate on his
sorrows. The poem moves from one contrasting element to
another while establishing a parallelism between Jovino's inner
world and the outer world of nature.

The second version is somewhat longer than the first. The
major novelty, however, is not the length, but the deliberate

depersonalization which strikes the reader in the later poem. Jovino, the transparent and unique pseudonym of Jovellanos, has been replaced by Fabio, a stock pseudonym of the Classical literary tradition. All mention of Enarda has disappeared, as has the story of the speaker's unfortunate love. His unhappiness and his desire for peace remain, but without concrete motivation. No memory of a specific woman, but only the metaphoric chain of slavery to "the world" is set against Fabio's longing for quietness. The emotional tension is thus less sharply defined.

The contrast between the two kinds of nature remains the same in the second version:

¡Ay, Anfriso, qué escenas a mis ojos,
cansados de llorar, presenta el cielo!
Rodeado de frondosos y altos montes
se extiende un valle, que de mil delicias
con sabia mano ornó Naturaleza.
Pártele en dos mitades, despeñado
de las vecinas rocas, el Lozoya,
por su pesca famoso y dulces aguas.
Del claro río sobre el verde margen
crecen frondosos álamos, que al cielo
ya erguidos alzan las plateadas copas,
o ya sobre las aguas encorvados,
en mil figuras miran con asombro
su forma en los cristales retratada.
De la siniestra orilla un bosque ombrío
hasta la falda del vecino monte
se extiende, tan ameno y delicioso,
que le hubiera juzgado el gentilismo
morada de algún dios, o a los misterios
de las silvanas dríadas guardado.
Aquí encamino mis inciertos pasos,
y en su recinto ombrío y silencioso,
mansión la más conforme para un triste,
entro a pensar en mi crüel destino.
La grata soledad, la dulce sombra,
el aire blando y el silencio mudo
mi desventura y mi dolor adulan.
*   No alcanza aquí del padre de las luces*
el rayo acechador, ni su reflejo
viene a cubrir de confusión el rostro
de un infeliz en su dolor sumido.
El canto de las aves no interrumpe
aquí tampoco la quietud de un triste,

pues sólo de la viuda tortolilla
se oye tal vez el lastimero arrullo,
tal vez el melancólico trinado
de la angustiada y dulce Filomena.
Con blando impulso el céfiro süave
las coplas de los árboles moviendo,
recrea el alma con el manso ruido;
mientras al dulce soplo desprendidas,
las agostadas hojas, revolando,
bajan en lentos círculos al suelo;
cúbrenle en torno, y la frondosa pompa
que al árbol adornara en primavera,
yace marchita, y muestra los rigores
del abrasado estío y seco otoño.
¡Así también de juventud lozana
pasan, oh Anfriso, las livianas dichas! (Pp. 183-84)

(What scenes, Anfriso, to my tear-worn eyes
does heaven present! High leafy hills ring in
a valley that by Nature's knowing hand
has been endowed with myriad delights.
Lozoya, rushing from the neighboring rocks,
divides it with its waters justly famed
for fish and purity, and on its banks
the leafy poplars raise their silvery tops,
or bending o'er the waters, see astonished
how in a thousand shapes the fleeting crystal
reflects their form. A shady forest lies
between the left bank and the nearby hill,
so pleasant and delightful that of old
men would have thought it dwelling of some god
or sacred to the cult of woodland dryads.
Here do I guide my faltering steps and enter
the shady silent space, fit home of sadness,
to ponder lonely my unhappy fate.
The pleasing solitude, the shade so sweet,
the gentle breeze, the silence—all combine
to soothe my sorrow, my unhappiness.
    The searching ray of the chief of all lights
does not reach here or bring a painful blush
to the unfortunate in sorrow sunk.
Neither does song of birds here interrupt
the sad man's quietness, for all he hears
is mournful cooing of the widowed dove
or melancholy trill of nightingale,
anguished and sweet. The kindly Zephyr moves
the treetops softly and with gentle sound

delights the soul, while by his sweet breath torn
loose from their branches, the parched leaves descend,
fluttering in slow circles, to the ground.
They cover it; and spring's bright leafy dress
lies wilted by hot summer and dry fall.
In this same way the frivolous delights
of our bright youth, Anfriso, pass away!)

The second version of the Epistle contains one element not present in the first: the exaltation of the life of a penitent monk, a tranquil and harmonious life which is contrasted with the troubled feelings, the sadness, and the terror of Fabio. Thus the internal emotional contrast, less clear in the second version than in the first, is partially replaced or supplemented by an external contrast between two types of life and two emotional states, represented by two separate figures.

Comparison of the two versions of this celebrated poem shows Jovellanos' tendency, characteristic of the philosophical and aesthetic trends of his time, to generalize and objectivize the originally subjective elements and to fit them into a scheme which would be universally applicable. Within the poem we also find the same alternation between general and particular, abstract and concrete, that marks the First Satire, written some seven years later. With the systematic suppression of the personal, the second version perhaps loses some of the immediacy and freshness of the first; yet it continues to be relatively rich in sensory images and in concrete language. It deserves the high place which criticism has traditionally assigned to it.

The description of nature also predominates in Jovellanos' Fifth Epistle, addressed to Meléndez and containing a sensory, historical, and religious appreciation of the Leonese countryside. In a more familiar and humorous vein, the Sixth Epistle describes the landscapes of León and Castile and contrasts them with the flourishing agricultural region of La Rioja. This contrast, in turn, leads Jovellanos to considerations reminiscent of his *Report on the Agrarian Law*, practically contemporary with this poem.

The subsequent epistles tend to abandon concrete language and to deal more with abstract philosophical themes, indicative of Jovellanos' ideological development, but usually not produc-

tive of first-rate poetry. An exception is the Tenth (and last)
Epistle (1807), addressed to Ceán Bermúdez during its author's
captivity in Majorca. It offers the reader examples of "the vain
desires and studies of men" in vigorous language reminiscent of
the satires. The poem's structure is well defined: after the introduction, Jovellanos deals with the vanity of human desires, then
stressing the importance of Virtue, which thus occupies the physical and philosophical center of the poem; this central section
is followed by exposition of the vanity of human studies, after
which the conclusion returns to the theme of virtue:

> Wisdom and happiness in virtue seek,
> for truth and virtue are the same, and they
> alone can give your soul a peace secure
> in purity of conscience, a true freedom
> in curbing your desires, and true joy
> in the sweet happiness of doing good.
> All else is wind and vanity and woe.

VII *Miscellaneous Verse Works*

Like all the poets of his time, Jovellanos wrote verses to com-
memorate such occasions as birthdays, weddings, and deaths.
These poems rely heavily on Classical mythology and allegory,
as did the graphic arts of the period; and their language tends to
be abstract. They do not display our author's poetic gifts to the
best advantage.

Different, and superior in the force of its sentiment and its
correspondingly vigorous rhythm is the "Asturian Battle Hymn"
urging resistance to Bonaparte. Jovellanos here employs strongly
dactylic ten-syllable verses with repeated assonance in final
stressed *o*. The eight-line strophe with four-line refrain had been
used by the eighteenth-century Italian poet Pietro Metastasio
and came, perhaps through the influence of Jovellanos, to be
current in Spanish and Spanish-American patriotic hymns. Specifically, Jovellanos' "Battle Hymn" inspired the Argentine
national anthem of Vicente López y Planes.[11]

In the 1770's Jovellanos rendered into Spanish verse two
fables by La Fontaine and Montesquieu's prose poem "Céphise
et l'Amour" ("Cephise and Eros"). His most ambitious effort in

translation, however, is a version in blank hendecasyllables of the first canto of Milton's *Paradise Lost*. Fragments of the same work were translated by Cadalso in his *Suplemento al papel intitulado Los eruditos a la violeta* (*Supplement to the Pamphlet Titled The Violet-Water Scholars*), 1772. Jovellanos began to work on his translation in Seville (Ceán, p. 293), that is, about the same time that Cadalso did; and his attention may have been drawn to the English poem by his poetic mentor. *Paradise Lost* continued to occupy Jovellanos for many years, as his interest in English letters and thought came to prevail over the French orientation of his youthful years in the circle of Olavide. In 1796 we find him polishing his translation; and in 1806, while a prisoner on Majorca, he delights in the receipt of an English-French bilingual edition of Milton (D II, 249; IV, 78b).

VIII   *Jovellanos as a Poet*

Jovellanos is not the major poet of his age, but he is an important one both for his influence on others and in himself. He contributed to the rise of a civic poetry that sang of patriotism, the betterment of mankind, virtue, and friendship. He led in the introduction of realistic themes developed in realistic language, a language which scandalized contemporary parlor poets. His poetic speech is highly flexible; the smoothly-flowing verse is often replaced by the broken line of interrogations and exclamations. It thus reclaims for poetry the rhythms of everyday speech, just as it often deals with the experiences of everyday life. This poetic trend, sometimes called "Enlightened" and sometimes "Pre-Romantic," culminated in Juan Meléndez Valdés and Nicasio Álvarez de Cienfuegos, both influenced by Jovellanos.[12] Jovellanos' letters testify to his constant concern with metrics; and although he made no technical innovations, "he gave new value to blank verse and to certain rhythmic elements of the hendecasyllable" (Caso, *Poesías*, pp. 54, 57).

Flexible rhythm and a broad concept of poetic language allow Jovellanos to achieve forceful expression; yet his flexibility does not become formlessness, as the careful structure of his works shows. These qualities of his verse are best combined in the satire, with its stress on morality, and in descriptions of nature. Both types of poetry concern themselves with topics close to Jovellanos' heart, and also important in his prose works. Although sincerity is the most overrated virtue, and in poetry, no virtue at all, Jovellanos' poetry is at its best when it springs from some enthusiasm—moral or aesthetic—and is then polished in subsequent periods of reflection. Polishing alone did not get Jovellanos beyond discreet mediocrity, as his amatory and occasional verses demonstrate.

Of the six poems that Jovellanos published in his lifetime, three—the first two satires and the "Epistle to Anfriso"—have won the acclaim of succeeding critics and literary historians of the most diverse schools, a percentage of successes which testifies to the author's good taste and poetic sensibility. Poetry, to be sure, was never the major concern of Jovellanos, a man for whom, at any rate, ethical considerations always outweighed the aesthetic; but it was a lasting concern, not only providing him with the pleasure of creation but also informing his vision of even the most mundane realities as he strove to bring a better life to his countrymen through a synthesis of the good and the beautiful.

CHAPTER 3

Drama

I *The Crisis of Eighteenth-Century Spanish Theater*

IN the late sixteenth and early seventeenth centuries, Spain produced a theater which in the quantity of its productions, their quality, and the permanence of their interest, is unequalled in Europe. The playwrights of this Golden Age drew their subject matter from many different sources and elaborated it in keeping with theatrical conventions which, though not codified in any ancient critical texts, gained authority from the example of that remarkable genius, Lope de Vega. Their plays contain three acts, employing a variety of verse forms and shifting from one form to another within the play according to recognizable patterns. They utilize certain stock themes (most notably, the defense of honor), attitudes, types of speeches, and motifs. Within these generally observed limits, the playwrights of Spain's Golden Age enjoyed great artistic freedom. They created a theater appealing to all classes and kinds of citizens and providing something for each and all: amusement, stimulation of thought, and aesthetic satisfaction. Furthermore, by presenting the glorious and heroic past of imperial and Catholic Spain, her equally glorious present, and the expectation of a likewise glorious future, many of these plays must have left their audiences with the comfortable feeling that God was in His heaven, the king on his throne, and all was right with the world. In some ways, then, this theater performed a social function analogous to that of the Hollywood movie before the invention of experimental films, problem films, protest films, and the like.

This type of play dominated the Spanish stage well into the eighteenth century, but by the late seventeenth century playwrights were turning the brilliant intuitions of their Golden Age predecessors into conventions. As the intrinsic originality of

their works decreased, they sought to maximize surprise and
shock; and their plays became more mannered and more
derivative, much as has happened with horror films produced
in imitation of such classics as *Dracula.*

It was with this theater that Ignacio de Luzán and his followers took issue, although their critical principles often brought
them also to attack the playwrights of the Golden Age. Luzán's
dramatic theory, expressed in Book III of his *Poetics,* stems
from Aristotle and Horace and their commentators, particularly
the Italian and the French. It emphasizes the social function of
art, the purity of literary genres, and the dramatic unities.

Luzán believed that theater, like all art, has a useful as well as
an ornamental social role. Tragedy, the more "noble" dramatic
genre, dealing with the passions of men of high estate, should
purge and refine emotions and provide instructive examples.
Comedy, dealing with the behavior of common men, should,
while amusing its audience, criticize abuses and thus further
their correction. Each genre has its function, its subject matter,
and its proper style (elevated for tragedy, plain for comedy);
and the two genres must not be blended in a single play, lest one
destroy the effect of the other. In order to maintain an illusion
of reality and thus further the pleasure and salutary instruction
of the spectator, all shocking inverisimilitude must be elimina-
ted. A play should therefore deal with a single main action, to
which any secondary actions are subordinated. It must avoid
startling shifts of scene, lest the spectator, realizing that he is
still sitting in the same theater, begin to reject the whole fictional apparatus. It must not claim for its action an extent of time
so manifestly out of keeping with the real time taken up by the
performance as to make the viewer escape completely from the
imaginary world of the stage.

We need not concern ourselves now with further details of
Luzán's dramatic theory. Its defects are those of all Neoclassic
theories: utilitarianism and lack of faith in the imagination of
the spectator. On the other hand, the famous unities do produce
a structural tightness that intensifies dramatic, and particularly
tragic, effect. These unities, furthermore, as well as the didactic
purpose of art, are rather liberally and intelligently interpreted
by Luzán.

The Golden Age produced few tragedies in the Neoclassic sense, since it mixed tragic elements with the comic, much as occurs in the tragedies of Shakespeare, Lope de Vega's contemporary. Golden Age comedy, furthermore, is not primarily, or even usually, critical of manners, as Neoclassical comedy ought to be. The unity of action is normally observed; but, again like the Shakespearean theater, the Golden Age pays no attention to the unities of time and place, ranging freely over the globe and the years in the course of a single play. Educated Spaniards of the eighteenth century saw that their national theater ignored the "rules" of drama accepted throughout Europe, and that much current production was of low quality by any standards. They were also aware of the ridicule liberally bestowed on them by foreigners. In France, Boileau had scornfully referred to the shocking excesses which might be committed only by "a rhymester from beyond the Pyrenees." The theater, in eighteenth-century Europe, was considered a touchstone of a nation's level of civilization and culture; and the Spaniards of that time, so open to foreign thought, were quick to develop a sense of their inferiority in this respect.

Luzán's ideas, vigorously discussed in the years following their publication, increasingly prevailed among Spain's intellectual elite. Not only were they accepted theoretically, but they stimulated efforts to create a "regular" theater, that is, a theater observant of the "rules" of Neoclassic drama. Most of the major literary figures of the middle and late eighteenth century were involved in this task: Luzán himself, author of Neoclassic comedies; Agustín Montiano y Luyando, a pioneer in the field of eighteenth-century tragedy; Nicolás Fernández de Moratín; Tomás de Iriarte, author of comedies of manners; Cadalso; Vicente García de la Huerta, author of the tragedy *Raquel* and defender of the Golden Age playwrights; and Leandro Fernández de Moratín, the son of Don Nicolás and author of various comedies, among them the justly famous *El sí de las niñas* (*A Maiden's Consent*).

Such efforts received support from a government concerned with cultural development. The ministers of Charles III prohibited the performance of the allegorical religious plays called *autos sacramentales* and of *comedias de santos*, whose saintly heroes, to the outrage of the more puritanical and less imaginative, were often portrayed by actors and actresses whose not-so-private lives fell a good deal short of sanctity. As first minister, the Count of Aranda also favored the Neoclassic cause by establishing theaters in the royal seats surrounding Madrid and commissioning for performance in them translations of "regular" foreign plays, mainly by French authors of the seventeenth and eighteenth centuries. These theaters, created in 1768, lasted about eight years; and the translations for them were, like the original dramas mentioned above, prepared by some of the main literary figures of the time.

II Pelayo

These are the literary and cultural circumstances under which Jovellanos, at the age of twenty-five, wrote his first known play, the tragedy *Pelayo*. The date of its original composition is 1769; it was subsequently revised by its author in 1771 and 1772 and was first performed by an amateur group in Gijón in 1782 (Ceán, pp. 306-9). Its action is set in Gijón in the early eighth century, not long after the Moslem conquest of Spain. Munuza, a Christian traitor whom the Moors have made governor of Gijón, has sent the noble Pelayo, nephew of the last Visigothic king of Spain, to Cordova, so that in his absence he may be able, by persuasion or by force, to marry Pelayo's sister, Dosinda, who has rejected him before. Dosinda, brought to Munuza's palace, continues to refuse his offers; and when Rogundo, her betrothed, protests against the governor's actions, he is arrested. Although urged by his counselor Achmet to avoid stirring up the brave and fierce Asturians, Munuza determines that the marriage is to take place that very day. Again he tries to persuade Dosinda, offering her the crown which he plans to seize for himself while his Moslem masters are busy fighting in France; but both she and Rogundo remain inflexible. At this point Pelayo, whom Munuza had wanted delayed in Cordova, unexpectedly appears. Spurning both the offers and the threats of Munuza, he threatens him with rebellion in turn. He convinces some citizens to join him in an uprising, and they proclaim him their king. Together they free Dosinda, who is being taken to church for her marriage to the governor. In the ensuing battle, Pelayo is captured; and refusing still to consent to his sister's marriage, he is condemned to die. Suddenly, however, the Asturians succeed in freeing the prisoners. In a great fight on stage, Achmet tries to protect Munuza from the enraged Rogundo but unwittingly causes his master's death. As the governor is carried off to die, the rebels, knowing that Moorish troops will soon come to Gijón, decide to leave for the mountains, where they will continue the struggle.

This subject is drawn from sources which Jovellanos himself considers largely apocryphal (I, 74, n. 3; II, 510) and on which his imagination has further embroidered. The figure of Pelayo is historical, and the historical sequel to the imaginary episode is known to every Spaniard: Pelayo's victory over the Moslems at Covadonga, the beginning of the Reconquest, completed by Ferdinand and Isabella in Granada on January 2, 1492. Jovellanos' play thus has a doubly patriotic appeal, Spanish and Asturian. In this it is characteristic of the Spanish Neoclassic tragedy, which consistently sought its subjects in the national past, particularly the medieval period, heroic, and also sufficiently remote to let the imagination play freely. Coupled with the historical research of such men as Father Enrique Flórez and with the publication of medieval Spanish poetry by Tomás Antonio Sánchez, this gives a picture of cultural continuity, in spite of the disputes about poetics, quite different from the systematic rejection of the national past, both historical and literary, which led the Neoclassicists of the French seventeenth century to people their stage with Versaillesque Greeks and Romans. Spain's Enlightenment and her Neoclassic literature have sometimes been falsely accused of being "antinational"; but the great minds of the period, while engaged in all kinds of reform, were devoted to the traditions of their country.

Jovellanos' *Pelayo* is written in eleven-syllable verses having assonant rhyme in the even-numbered lines, a form called *romance heroico* and employed in several Neoclassic tragedies. The weighty, solid, eleven-syllable verses produce the effect of seriousness and deliberateness appropriate to a tragedy, while the vowel rhymes, at a distance of twenty-two syllables, create a diluted musicality. The rhymed couplet, used by Cadalso in what seems to be imitation of the French playwrights, was never able to conquer the Spanish stage.

The action of *Pelayo* fits rather well within the limits of a single day, its antecedents being narrated in conversations between the main characters and their confidants, as is common in much Neoclassic theater. It takes place in different parts of Munuza's palace, adhering to a liberal interpretation of the unity of place. It concerns a single event, Munuza's attempt to force a marriage with Dosinda and the consequent beginning of Christian resistance to Moorish domination; and there is no secondary action whatsoever. The characters—of royal or noble blood, or, in Munuza's case, of elevated station—are of a rank deemed suitable for tragedy in Neoclassic dramatic theory.

That theory also demanded that the tragic hero be a mixture of good and evil, neither a wholly innocent victim nor a scoundrel fully deserving of his destruction. Only in this way can the desired effect of pity and terror be produced; and only in this way can the spectator feel that the tragic hero is worthy of compassion, and, at the same time, that his fate confirms the existence of moral laws whose fulfillment is also a source of satisfaction—a combination of sentiments which constitutes the tragic emotion.

Among the characters of *Pelayo*, the most complex and most interesting, though not the most admirable, is Munuza. He has betrayed his people and his religion and now rules over them for a foreign master. He claims, however, that Visigothic Spain was lost because of the wrongdoings of her monarchs (an allusion to the story of King Roderick and his sinful amours with La Cava), and that he has cast his lot with the conquerors only in order better to serve his people (I, 70b). Munuza has favored Pelayo, a descendant of the dethroned dynasty whom he has every reason to fear and whose friendship is not likely to meet with the approval of his masters. Pelayo himself, however, insists that he has never sought the friendship of Munuza; and he refuses to believe the motives which Munuza alleges for his treason. Munuza, then, occupies an ambiguous political position, for reasons which are also ambiguous or conflicting.

The same complexity underlies Munuza's effort to marry Dosinda. His passion is only in part amorous; his ambition leads him to covet a crown which, he believes, will fit his head more readily if he is married to a member of the royal house (I, 61b). His pride makes him persist in the effort once undertaken; since all know of his desires, retreat would be an intolerable humiliation (I, 62). In the final scenes, Munuza refuses to seek safety in flight; he is prepared to face Pelayo, preferring death to shame. Even as he dies, he calls Pelayo "traitor" and accuses an "unjust heaven" of his fate. He never admits that he has acted wrongly.

At times Munuza seems to be a strong man enslaved by his passions and thus a fit subject for tragedy, which, in Neoclassic theory, is to deal with just such cases. He ultimately dies because of his own wrongdoing, his attempt to force Dosinda to marry him; yet this wrongdoing is motivated by the passions of love and ambition, both, perhaps, culpable in this instance, yet neither of them low or abominable in itself. Not unreasonably was the play sometimes called *Munuza*. Pelayo, whose name Jovellanos uses as the title of his tragedy, does not appear on stage until past the middle of the third act (the play has five). Munuza fills the stage from beginning to end. Yet the "terror" which one feels at his fall is checked by the patriotic exultation of Pelayo and his men, and by doubts about how great Munuza was to begin with. The pity aroused by his fate is likewise limited, since the evil, or at least ambiguous, in him outweighs the good and noble.

Munuza, then, is not a successful Neoclassic hero. In more modern terms, however, he lives the tragedy of an essentially small man buffeted by events great beyond his capacity. He compares himself to a "fragile reed" that bends with the storm (I, 70b). He is not of noble Gothic blood, as Pelayo takes pains to remind him in his indignation at the proposed marriage: "You, in plebeian darkness born to serve / under my laws . . ." (I, 65a). Munuza "bends" with the Moslem invasion, and the situation in which he consequently finds himself breeds in him the ambition of a throne and of a royal bride. Yet he does not have the capacity to live with these circumstances. He does not act ruthlessly or rapidly enough to get his way; and even while he is trying to do so, he craves the approval of Dosinda, of Pelayo, and even of the Rogundo whom he is trying to replace

in Dosinda's affections. But he fails in all his efforts at persuasion. He cannot overcome the stains of his birth and his betrayal
of his country and his faith, and he is repeatedly spurned by
those whose favor he implores.

In Jovellanos' eyes, Pelayo is probably the hero of the play.
The spectator is to fear Pelayo's dishonor and even death; and
the happy outcome of his difficulties does not disqualify him as
a tragic hero in Neoclassic theory, which allows for "happy-
ending" tragedies. The important thing is that the vicissitudes of
an elevated character arouse terror and pity in the spectator, re-
gardless of whether the eventual solution is happy or, as is more
customary, unhappy. Jovellanos would also expect the spectator to pity Pelayo in his difficulties; but this pity would be
limited, especially today, when Pelayo's arrogance of caste
would not arouse much sympathy.

Pelayo's difficulties stem from his friendship with Munuza,
which encouraged the governor to consider a marriage with
Dosinda as something not impossible. Why, however, did Pelayo
allow this friendship to develop if he believed Munuza to be as
vile as he now asserts him to be? Surely not for his own aggran-
dizement; yet if he accepted a vile friendship only in order to
protect his people under Munuza's rule, is that not the same
kind of reasoning with which Munuza justifies his collaboration
with the Moors? And if Pelayo is really only now finding out
the vileness of his friend, this vileness must consist chiefly of
the personal affront of aspiring to marry Pelayo's sister, because all the previous actions of Munuza, including his betrayal,
were known to Pelayo. Whatever the case, Pelayo's troubles are
of ignoble origin.

Pelayo's harangue to his followers (I, 65b-66a) does not make
him appear in a more favorable light. He warns them of the
imminent loss of their liberty and paints for them a picture of
their women being transported into the harems of the infidels,
and their churches being turned into mosques. Yet in the past
years of Moslem domination none of this has happened. Apart
from these fancied terrors, then, the only concrete and immediate danger is Munuza's intended marriage with Dosinda, which
Pelayo views as a double insult: a violation of an engagement
and an affront to his royal blood. Historically, Pelayo is the

greatest personage of the tragedy; but within the play, he is less interesting and even less noble than his antagonist.

Dosinda and Rogundo are undeveloped characters whose only discernible traits are inflexible fidelity to each other and a consequently inflexible resistance to the threats and blandishments of Munuza. Jovellanos' explanation of Rogundo reflects the theories of Montesquieu on the different forms of government and the influence of climate and other natural factors on social institutions: "This honorable delicacy with which Rogundo forestalls the tyrant's ideas, and the steadfastness with which he later rejects his offers, reveal the full character of a noble descendant of the Goths, born in a temperate climate and reared under a monarchical government [whose guiding principle, according to Montesquieu, is honor] and a martial legislation" (I, 76, n. 26). Of the four other named characters—and the small number of personages is in itself characteristic of the Neoclassic theater—three are confidants who, in conversations with their masters, explain the situation and its antecedents. Concerning one of these confidants, the Moor Achmet, Jovellanos makes the following remark, in keeping with the ideology of the Enlightenment: "We have given this personage, who is also episodic, an honest character, a proceeding which will perhaps surprise those who are used to seeing our playwrights always depict all the adherents of other religions in dark and abominable colors. But we have not wished to imitate them . . ." (I, 75, n. 12).

The plot of *Pelayo* follows the traditional Neoclassic line of development: exposition in the first act; increased difficulties in the second and third; a turn for the better in the third and fourth, as Pelayo returns and there is hope of rescuing Dosinda, and then a double turnabout in the fifth act, as the rebels first seem defeated, with Pelayo a prisoner, and then succeed after all, and Munuza is killed. This solution, resting on the outcome of an offstage battle, does not flow naturally from the moral qualities of the characters. It is contrived to let Pelayo go forward to those victories which the audience knows lie in store for him.

Although *Pelayo* has some stage indications calling for physical acts, largely by the women, who are to express sadness in their faces and postures and who on occasion are to fall and

faint, its action advances primarily through dialogue. This dialogue tends to consist more of speeches than of unstrained
conversation; but such artificiality is not necessarily a defect in
Neoclassic drama, which strives, particularly in tragedy, for a
stylized, often almost ritual, effect. There are a few lapses
in the rhyme pattern, but the modern reader is perhaps more
disturbed by the scarcity of moving or lyrical passages. Each
speech has its function within the play; but few have the intrinsic merit of this description of the Asturians, no doubt inspired
by the author's patriotic sentiments:

> Well do you know these brave and fierce men's ardor.
> Leaping and fighting are the sports of those
> born midst the rocks. Sometimes they test their strength
> casting with robust hand enormous trunks
> as though they were a light and easy weight.
> The beasts in the high mountains do they track,
> then conquer them and take away their young.
> As pastime always armed with knotty clubs,
> habitual to them, on the foe they rush;
> and to safeguard their liberty and laws,
> rather would they choose death than a defeat.
> Ferocious virtue, common to them all! (I, 60b-61a)

There are occasional lapses in diction, such as *que puede ser que
con el tiempo sea / de nuestra libertad tu sangre el precio* ("for
it may well be that your blood in time / may come to be the
price of liberty"), I, 60a.

Jovellanos claims that his *Pelayo* follows such French models
as Racine and Voltaire rather than Greek or Latin tragedies (I,
51; Caso, *Poesías*, p. 110). Of the two French playwrights,
Voltaire probably is more influential than Racine. It is hard to
find tragic grandeur in *Pelayo*, but the appeal to patriotism is
certainly useful in Jovellanos' eyes. In a verse prologue which he
wrote for the 1782 performance of *Pelayo*, the author stresses
his patriotic inspiration and the need to celebrate the glories of
the national past, a need which he had also emphasized in his
epistle to the Salamancans. He declares Pelayo to be the main
figure of his play; and he evokes Greek and Latin models, with
no mention now of the French (Caso, *Poesías*, pp. 200-203).

Pelayo was first performed in Gijón in 1782, and there was a
performance in Madrid in 1792.[1] According to Ceán (pp. 306-

9), Jovellanos planned to publish the tragedy in 1773, when he wrote notes and a prose prologue for it; but the publication was not to take place in the author's lifetime. In 1814 there appeared a considerably altered version, entitled *Munuza* (I, 52, n. 1); but the first printing of the authentic text came in Volume VI of the Cañedo edition of Jovellanos' works (Madrid, 1832).

III   *Translations and a Second Tragedy*

About the same time that Jovellanos was writing *Pelayo*, he was also translating Racine's *Iphigénie* for performance in the royal theaters. These were established by Aranda in the same year that the minister met the young Asturian and favored him with a position in Seville. Olavide, Jovellanos' superior in Seville, was translating several plays for the same theaters; and Jovellanos naturally participated in the enterprise.[2] The text of his version, however, is not known to us. Subsequently, probably after 1775, Jovellanos began an original tragedy entitled *Los españoles en Cholula* (*The Spaniards in Cholula*), apparently dealing with the conquest of Mexico and thus in keeping with the author's ideas on a theater celebrating the glories of the national past. The text of this unfinished play is also lost (Ceán, pp. 311-12; Caso, *Poesías*, p. 444, n. 43). Although Jovellanos never wrote another tragedy, his interest in doing so remained alive; in 1795 he is still intrigued by the tragic possibilities of a Greek history that he is reading (D II, 191-92).

IV   El delincuente honrado (The Honorable Culprit)

The autobiographical poem "Historia de Jovino" ("History of Jovino") indicates that Jovellanos cultivated comedy before writing *Pelayo* (Caso, *Poesías*, p. 110 and n. 44), but either he destroyed his texts or they were otherwise lost. Jovellanos' only extant play other than *Pelayo* is often, albeit loosely, ascribed to the comic genre; but it is later than *Pelayo.*

This play is *El delincuente honrado* (*The Honorable Culprit*), written in 1773. Early in that year, in the circle of Don Pablo de Olavide in Seville, there arose a discussion concerning the merits of prose tragicomedy or sentimental comedy; and although, in keeping with sound Neoclassic doctrine, it was agreed that such plays were an unnatural mixture of the two standard genres, several of those present decided to write a play each in this new fashion. Jovellanos' contribution, *The Honorable Culprit*, was judged the best of all; and it is the only one to have survived. It was first performed in 1774 in one of the royal theaters; having been written in prose, it underwent versification at the hands of several volunteers and was translated into various foreign languages; and, after a pirated edition appeared in Barcelona, it was pseudonymously published by its author in Madrid in 1787 (Ceán, pp. 312-13; I, 77).

In *The Honorable Culprit*, Torcuato, a young man of obscure ancestry, intolerably provoked by a nobleman, had agreed to meet him in a secret and illegal duel, in the course of which the nobleman has literally rushed upon Torcuato's sword and died. Torcuato has subsequently married his victim's widow, Laura, encouraged by her father, who appreciates his virtues and, like Laura, knows nothing of Torcuato's participation in the duel. With the arrival of an investigating judge determined to discover the truth about the nobleman's death, the hero decides to flee; yet when his friend Anselmo is arrested for the crime, Torcuato confesses and, in keeping with the law, is condemned to death by the judge, Don Justo de Lara, who subsequently turns out to be his father. At the last minute, and after he has been led out to execution, Torcuato is saved by word that the king has commuted his sentence to banishment.

The play seems to be based on an actual event which occurred in Segovia, the scene of its action, in 1758.[3] There are also thematic and onomastic similarities with an episode from Roman history narrated by Livy, in which Torquatus Manlius condemns his own son for violating a prohibition against single combat with the enemy.[4]

The action of Jovellanos' play is one and undivided, its purpose being "to show the harshness of the laws which inflict capital punishment on duelists without distinguishing between the provoked and the provoker" (I, 79). It takes some twenty-eight to thirty hours of fictional time; and, like *Pelayo*, it occurs in different parts of a single building, in this case the Alcázar of Segovia. The adherence to a strict concept of the unities is thus fairly unstrained, if one is willing to accept the severity of a legal process that discovers a culprit, sentences him the same day, and leads him out to his death the next morning. There are, however, other flaws in the play's verisimilitude. Is it really likely that Don Simón, a magistrate "of the old school," would actively promote the marriage of his daughter to a man of unknown family?[5] Can one believe that Don Justo, knowing that Anselmo has gone to implore the mercy of the king, and with his own son's life at stake, would order Torcuato's execution without even waiting to hear the outcome of Anselmo's errand?[6] These are problems brought about by the way Jovellanos conceives his plot, and which he has not taken the trouble to resolve.

The conflict in *The Honorable Culprit* is not an inner moral one, and Jovellanos' concern with other aspects of the play may explain his sometimes scant attention to the motivation of his characters. Torcuato prepares to leave his wife, stays and confesses his guilt in order to save his friend, accepts his condemnation, and accepts his suddenly-revealed father, all without inner struggle and always in total subjection to his ideas of duty. Similarly, Don Justo, although he considers the law on duels unjust, unhesitatingly condemns Torcuato. After he has discovered that the culprit is his son, he remains determined to carry out the law to its full extent. Virtue seems inevitably to triumph in these characters; and their virtue is of the inflexible kind that makes some Roman heroes so admirable and so inhuman. In Jovellanos' characters, the triumph of virtue is accompanied by full consciousness of the sacrifices involved; the author, however, does not use this consciousness to study an emotional process, but to enhance a pathos expressed in sentimental scenes and in the copious shedding of tears.

As I have written elsewhere,

the basic conflict of the play must . . . be sought on a level entirely different from the sentimental one . . . Jovellanos establishes a contrast between two concepts of the law, embodied in two magistrates, Don Justo and Don Simón, the *corregidor*. Don Justo is "a philosophical magistrate, that is, enlightened, virtuous, and humane," while Don Simón, "a slave to common prejudices, and endowed with a limited talent and education, ignorantly approves whatever the laws provide, and condemns without examining it whatever is contrary to them" (I, 79). In other words, Simón is unable to rise to a philosophic level on which he can judge not only individuals but also laws and institutions; his criteria are totally formalistic, and he accepts as valid whatever has been decreed by constituted authority. This position is in conflict with Justo's, since Justo not only judges individual guilt by legal standards, but also examines these standards themselves in the light of ethical principles. He is, therefore, both a minister and a critic of the society he serves; and through him Jovellanos expresses his demand for the adjustment of legal to ethical values. Don Simón is the foil to these opinions and consequently one of the major characters in the ideological struggle, although in the Torcuato-plot his role is secondary. His opinions and Justo's increase the piquancy of their situations. Simón finds that the man whose death he has so eagerly demanded is his son-in-law; Justo is forced to condemn his son in the name of a law which punishes alike the provoker and the provoked in a duel, and which, as a "philosophical magistrate," he considers unjust. Royal intervention supports Justo's philosophy of law and the lesson which Simón has been forced to learn; but let us note that the king is not moved by reason, but by the pathetic plea of Torcuato's friend, Anselmo. In a most "Enlightened" fashion, royal sentimentality tempers royal rigor.[7]

Jovellanos points out a discrepancy between the real standards of society and the laws which supposedly embody those standards. Through his characters, he admits that the prevalent concept of honor is "false," ignoring, as it does, a man's inner worth; but he claims that when such a concept is widely held and, in effect, is the fundamental principle of the monarchical government under which the characters live, the law must not punish men for obeying a code which society would punish them for violating. Accepting a duel should be no crime for the provoked party when his refusal would bring him the contempt of his fellow citizens and make him an outcast in their eyes. This argument can be found in Hobbes and in such writers of the Enlightenment as Montesquieu and the Italian legal reformer Cesare Beccaria, whom Jovellanos quotes at the end of his play.[8] The solution to the conflict in *The Honorable Culprit* is a *deus*—or *rex—ex machina*, dramatically as unmotivated as the ending of those Golden Age works in which the king appears to deal out justice and decree the necessary marriages, or, for that matter, as the ending of *Pelayo*.

Apart from any real event and from the writings of Enlightenment "philosophers," the sources of *The Honorable Culprit* must be sought in French dramatic theory and practice of the eighteenth century, especially the dramatic theories of Denis

Diderot, developed in the *Entretiens sur le Fils naturel* (*Conversations about The Natural Son*) and *De la Poésie dramatique* (*On Dramatic Poetry*). In these works, Diderot explains what had already been practiced by him and other French playwrights, something which he calls a new theatrical genre, "the serious genre." Diderot had no aesthetic quarrel with most of the "rules" of Neoclassic theater, including the dramatic unities; but he wished to give theater a stronger social orientation. To this intent he proclaimed new rules of his own. The new genre was to deal with important subjects in simple and realistic plots, carrying on the action by means of the principal personages and dispensing with the valets so important in French comedy. It would scorn sensationalism and laughter and seek rather to work on the sentiments of its audience through moving scenes produced by the physical arrangement of the actors (*tableaux*). Pantomime, or the development of the action through gesture and movement, was to enhance the realism and, in some instances, the sentimental force of the play. At all times was there to be a strongly moral orientation. Finally, the drama would be based on social condition, not on character.[9]

Specifically, Diderot recommends that "someone set out to present on the stage the condition of the judge. Let him develop his plot in as interesting a manner as it allows. . . . Let his man be forced by the functions of his calling, either to betray the dignity and sanctity of his office, and to be dishonored in the eyes of others and his own, or to sacrifice his own passions, his tastes, his fortune, his birth, his wife, and his children; and then anyone who cares to may say that the proper and serious drama lacks warmth, color and force."[10]

Jovellanos' play follows these suggestions and rules. It deals with important subjects, intensely debated even today: not only the justness or unjustness of laws, but also the duty of the citizen (Torcuato) and the magistrate toward a law which they consider unjust. The plot, though not very simple, is more so than that of any comedy of intrigue; and in spite of lapses in verisimilitude, it is realistic in its precisely-described setting, in dealing with a real and not a farfetched problem, in using ordinary characters, and in using prose, albeit a sometimes rhythmic, quasipoetic prose.[11] The action is carried on among the principal characters, with next to no occasion for laughter. Furthermore, "the movements of Torcuato in the first act, indicative of his troubled state of mind; the tears; the groupings and movements of characters in the fourth and fifth acts, with Torcuato in chains, in the dark prison area; the pleas and posturings of Laura; and the final release and embraces—all develop plot through action, movement, pantomime, and set up scenes designed to be visually impressive: *tableaux*" (Polt, *"Delincuente,"* p. 181). There is no need to underline the moral orientation of the play. As for the role of social condition,

Don Justo seems made to comply with Diderot's request; his conflict is precisely that envisaged by the latter: the human emotions of the man opposed by the sacred obligations of the judge. Justo lives fully his social role, his *condition*, that of judge; hence the poignancy of his being compelled to condemn his own long-lost son. But the same importance of *condition* is also to be found in the characterization of Torcuato, with a slightly more complex grouping of roles: husband, friend, virtuous citizen, and criminal. The play's title indicates at once that the conflict of the play rests on the paradoxical nature of this combination. . . . The characters do not seem to have any core of personality; rather they slip suddenly and sharply from one role into another, always fitting perfectly the preconceived norms of that role. Their personalities have facets, but no depth; like the title, they remain at the stage of unresolved paradox. It would seem that Jovellanos, moving from the abstract plane to the concrete, set up opposing concepts (husband, judge, father, etc.) and gave them names, rather than imagining the person and moving outward from a well-defined personality. The modern reader, always interested in psychological penetration, will find this unsatisfactory; Jovellanos' audience, far less interested in psychology than in the sociology that passed as "philosophy," apparently approved. Once more, what may to us seem a defect in the play should rather be viewed as conscious conformity with a dramatic theory, Diderot's. (*Ibid.*, p. 182)

Although author and critics vacillated concerning the genre of the play, *The Honorable Culprit* is, in fact, a Spanish representative of the middle-class theater which the French called *drame.*

Besides providing the theoretical basis of the play, Diderot and other French authors of the same tendency, writing in the 1750's, 1760's, and early 1770's, are also the sources of several details of plot and expression in *The Honorable Culprit.* In addition to Diderot's *Le Fils naturel* (*The Natural Son*), one must consider plays by Michel-Jean Sedaine, Sébastien Mercier, and Fenouillot de Falbaire, whose *L'Honnête criminel* (*The Honest Criminal*) bears a title mirrored in *The Honorable Culprit.* Both plays, however, like the anonymous *Honnête voleur* (*The Honest Thief*), may simply testify to the popularity of paradoxical titles, contemporaneous with the literary rehabilitation of the criminal.[12]

The Honorable Culprit achieved instant and long-lasting popularity. It seems to have been translated into French, English, German, and Italian; at least the Italian, and possibly the German and English versions also, were printed (Caso, "Delincuente," p. 105 and n. 4). In 1796 two hundred copies of the play were sent to the Philippines (D II, 245). An American edition was published in New York in 1829. Performances in Madrid were fairly frequent from 1791 to 1819 (Coe, *passim*), and in the 1830's the play is mentioned as still current, in articles by Ramón de Mesonero Romanos ("La comedia casera" ["The Amateur Performance"]) and Mariano José de Larra ("Yo quiero ser cómico" ["I Want to be an Actor"]). Cándido Nocedal (born in 1821) saw it performed in his childhood (I, xi); and though by 1845 it had disappeared from the Spanish stage,[13] this is a very respectable three score and ten years after its composition. Its vogue continued in Spanish America, where it was performed as late as 1852.[14]

Furthermore, *The Honorable Culprit,* though the best known, is not the only specimen of the new genre. Cándido María Trigueros, a very minor literary figure of the latter eighteenth century, composed *Los menestrales* (*The Workmen*), 1781, a social drama highly praised by Jovellanos (II, 163b). In 1796 Juan Pablo Forner published and presented on the stage *La escuela de la amistad o el filósofo enamorado* (*The School of Friendship, or The Philosopher in Love*), the prologue to which defends serious comedy. Forner's verse play abounds in pantomime and is adequately supplied with tears. Even the dramatic school of Comella, usually thought of as the degenerate rear guard of the Golden Age tradition, produced a number of such plays, including two imitations of the *Culprit* by Antonio Valladares y Sotomayor.[15] The outstanding Neoclassical comediographer, Leandro Fernández de Moratín, is indebted to the new school and to its pioneering play, *The Honorable Culprit.* His masterpiece, *A Maiden's Consent* (1801), has a strong social thesis, like the new dramas (see Caso, "Delincuente," p. 123); furthermore, it is a prose play in which the conflict is resolved by a sentimental virtue that finds full expression in the *tableau* of the last scene.

There are resemblances between Jovellanos' play and the Romantic theater: the recurrent sentimentality, the use of prose, the hero's view of himself as the victim of a hostile fate; yet Romantic theater lacked the social orientation of the eighteenth-century drama. While the latter made certain formal innovations so that it would better serve its social role of useful instruction, Romanticism quarreled with Neoclassicism on aesthetic grounds, something that did not occur to Diderot and his followers. There is greater similarity between the eighteenth-century drama and the "serious" or "high" comedy of the second half of the nineteenth century, represented in Spain by such playwrights as Adelardo López de Ayala and Manuel Tamayo y Baus; but it is not clear what relationship, if any, there is between these two dramatic schools.

V *Other Dramatic Efforts*

Although Jovellanos continued to take an active interest in the theater, no text remains that would allow us to judge his efforts. He planned a comedy which, using humble characters in an Asturian setting, would deal with marriage between partners of widely disparate ages, the theme repeatedly and successfully used by Leandro de Moratín; but we have only the résumé of this play and the outlines of some of its scenes (Caso, "Delincuente," pp. 131-32, n. 26). Jovellanos' diary of the 1790's refers to "El regocijo" ("The Rejoicing"), "Los alumnos" ("The Pupils"), and *El agradecimiento* (*Gratitude*), all of them, it seems, brief allegorical playlets related to the life of the Royal Asturian Institute. The manuscript of the second was preserved in Gijón but presumably destroyed during the Civil War in 1936; according to one authority, its author was not Jovellanos.[16] The third was apparently printed in Oviedo.[17] From Jovellanos' diary it is clear only that he made corrections and improvements in these small pieces and was involved in their performance, but not that he was their author. Among Don Gaspar's extant works, a fragment of a dialogue on economic subjects, while composed to be read, also uses the dramatic form (V, 146 ff.).

CHAPTER 4

The Arts: Historical and Critical Writings

I *Principal Works*

H IS diary shows Jovellanos to be a constant observer of land-scapes and of architectural and artistic monuments; and he deals with aesthetic, and particularly literary, questions in letters and numerous other works. Important among these are the *Memoria para el arreglo de la policía de los espectáculos y diversiones públicas, y sobre su origen en España (Report on the Regulation of Spectacles and Public Entertainments and on their Origin in Spain)*, 1790, *Reglamento para el Colegio de Calatrava (Regulations for the College of Calatrava)*, 1790, *Tratado teórico-práctico de enseñanza (Theoretical-Practical Treatise on Educa-tion)*, 1802, and *Curso de humanidades castellanas (Course in Spanish Humanities)*, 1794?, which, though of doubtful author-ship, reflects Jovellanos' pedagogical and aesthetic ideas.

Jovellanos also devoted a number of longer essays specifically to art and architecture. Shortly after his arrival in Madrid he read his *Elogio de las bellas artes (In Praise of the Fine Arts)*, 1781, which traces the development of the arts in Spain from Classical antiquity until the eighteenth century. Adhering close-ly to Neoclassical canons of taste, Jovellanos sees in Antiquity an aesthetic high point which, after periods of corruption, art seeks to regain. Toward the end of his Madrid period, Jovellanos wrote his *Elogio de Ventura Rodríguez (Eulogy of Ventura Rodríguez)*, 1788, sketching the life of the celebrated eight-eenth-century architect. In the author's view of architectural history, Rodríguez is a restorer of good taste after the corrup-tion of the Baroque. This *Eulogy* was published in 1790 with twenty notes, more extensive than the text and of greater gen-eral interest, elaborating the outline of architectural history given in the 1781 essay on the fine arts.

Although Jovellanos' interest in the arts and architecture was lifelong, his writings on these subjects are most abundant between 1805 and 1808, during the time of his captivity in the castle of Bellver, on Majorca. Three factors spurred this activity: abundant leisure, the need for distraction, and the desire to help the art historian Ceán Bermúdez, to whom these writings are addressed. The *Memoria del Castillo de Bellver, descripción histórico-artística*, or simply *Descripción del Castillo de Bellver* (*Essay on the Castle of Bellver: an Historical-Artistic Description*, or *Description of the Castle of Bellver*), deals with the castle outside Palma and the geology, flora, fauna, and popular festivals of the surrounding region, besides evoking scenes from Bellver's past. In an appendix, *Memorias del castillo de Bellver* (*Memoir of the Castle of Bellver*), we follow the history of the building from its foundation in the early fourteenth century until the mid-eighteenth century.

The *Descripción panorámica del castillo de Bellver* (*A Panorama from the Castle of Bellver*) observes the landscape from the homage tower of the castle, a viewpoint to which the author alludes frequently. Two essays, printed as appendices to the *Description of the Castle of Bellver*, are really appendices to the *Panorama*, because they deal in detail with buildings that the *Panorama* views from a distance: the convents of St. Dominic and St. Francis and the *lonja*, or mercantile exchange, of Palma. Both appendices consist of architectural and historical notes in which Jovellanos' admiration for the fifteenth-century Gothic *lonja* and for its architect, Guillermo Sagrera, is particularly evident. Confined to Bellver, Jovellanos employed an assistant to study these other buildings and to copy relevant documents, while he read Majorcan histories on the period of their construction (I, 431b, 433a).

The interesting essay *Sobre la arquitectura inglesa y la llamada gótica* (*On English and So-Called Gothic Architecture*), also known as *Carta de Philo Ultramarino* (*Letter from Philo Ultramarinus*, that is, from a Friend Beyond the Sea—Jovellanos himself, on Majorca), gives a résumé of Jean-Louis Ferri de Saint Constant's book on *Londres et les anglais* (*London and the English*), Paris, 1804, followed by Jovellanos' own reflections on English and Gothic architecture, picturesque beauty, landscape gardening, and English aesthetics and art. Finally, the *Descripción de la catedral de Palma* (*Description of the Cathedral of Palma*) is, more than a description of this Gothic edifice, a history of its foundation, construction, patrons, and architects.

II   *General Considerations*

Jovellanos' aesthetic ideas evolved with the trends of his time and were, to some extent, in their forefront. One of the principal questions which concerned Neoclassic aesthetics was the relationship between art and nature, taking "nature" to mean the world as created by God, as opposed to the work created by the artist. "Nature," then, is "reality"; and art, for the Neoclassicist, was imitation of nature according to principles derived from nature itself, codified in rules, and buttressed by the authority of the Ancients. As one of the leading thinkers of the Enlightenment, Condillac, put it, "Art is nothing but the collection of the rules which we need for learning to do something" (*L'Art d'écrire, Œuvres,* VII [Paris, 1798], 390). For Jovellanos also, art is "the collection of rules established for doing something well" (D I, 375). These rules and principles, he believed, are "taken from nature, in which are found all models of the sublime, the beautiful, and the graceful" (I, 497b); and additional guidance comes from observation of how the Ancients imitated nature (I, 362, n. 35). "Idealistic" art, which "imitates" the constructs or ideas of the mind rather than any real objects existing in nature, can therefore never be fully successful, because it departs from the models of nature. Medieval art, for instance, could not progress, Jovellanos believed, because it did not follow "a fixed and definite system of proportions" (I, 352a), that is, the proportions of nature. Jovellanos rejects what strikes us as modern in much medieval painting: a system of proportions that reflects not natural facts but concepts (a king is bigger than a servant), and the juxtaposition in the same pictorial space of scenes widely separated in space or time.

Aesthetic pleasure, according to Jovellanos, springs from the perception of perfection. The pleasure to be derived from art is therefore greater than that which can be derived from nature, because the work of art involves two separate perfections, that of the object imitated and that of the imitation (I, 265b).

The enjoyment of natural beauty presented a theoretical problem for Neoclassicism. Nature had no discernible rules and was often asymmetrical or apparently chaotic. Why is a gnarled, seemingly ill-proportioned tree, for instance, pleasing to the eye? Why are some faces attractive even though they do not adhere to the established canons of beauty? Feijóo attacked this problem in an article entitled "El no sé qué" ("The Certain Something"), explaining that beauty which seems to defy the "rules of art" stems from adherence to a superior order of rules not discernible by ordinary men. Symmetry, proportion, and order thus continue to be the guarantees of aesthetic pleasure; but genius, and even more the supreme genius of God as manifested in nature, discovers this harmony, perhaps intuitively, on a level beyond the comprehension of common mortals, though the results are not beyond their appreciation.

The question increased in importance as the eighteenth century drew to a close. Sentiment came to be prized as highly as reason, spontaneity as highly as discipline, and the charming disorder of nature as highly as an ordered rational art. In 1782, Jovellanos asked: "And are there fools art's beauties to prefer, / from you, oh Nature, never copied well, / to you yourself, their source and sacred pattern?" (Caso, *Poesías*, p. 195). On Majorca, twenty years later, even while exalting the unique pleasure to be derived from art, he shows an increasing awareness of paradoxically "irregular" beauty in both nature and art, and in the blending of the two. He enjoys viewing the architectural monuments of Palma with a mind free of the rules of art (I, 391); and he appreciates a scene of ruins and decay which would in future years appeal to the Romantics: "The vegetable kingdom produced by the castle, if not more fertile [than the animal kingdom], is more varied and noteworthy; and it both speeds its decay and makes its appearance more pleasing and picturesque" (I, 397b).

During this period Jovellanos came into contact with the English school of picturesque beauty represented by William Gilpin, which sought to combine nature with art and to give a place not only to the well-proportioned and conventionally pleasing, but also to the wild, the rare, the horrid, and the sublime. This aesthetics manifested itself especially in the English garden or park, planned to produce sentiments and emotions in the beholder, and thus differing from the geometric French garden, abstract, rationally perceived rather than "felt." Jovellanos now criticized both of the dominant aesthetic schools of his time. The *naturalists* could not surpass the beauty of the nature they sought to imitate (the beauty of the imitation itself seems now to be forgotten). On the other hand, the *idealists* imitated the Ancients rather than nature and therefore lacked force and truth in their works. The modern English, however, in Jovellanos' view, went beyond these schools. They had a broader concept of beauty than did the Ancients, who largely confined themselves to the animated human figure. They recognized, both in the Ancients and in nature, different kinds of beauty; and not content with copying nature, they improved it. The English, therefore, seemed to Jovellanos the people most likely to reach perfection in the arts.[1]

An approach to Pre-Romantic aesthetics, while unformulated, is already discernible in the scenes of gloom and horror of the epistle to the Salamancans and the "Epistle from Fabio to Anfriso." During his Majorcan years, Jovellanos is pleased to see it acquire form and formulation in the work of Gilpin and in the English garden-park, yet he does not abandon his fundamental utilitarianism. Beauty, he believes, should be combined with usefulness; and of the two, usefulness, as in the construction of roads, bridges, schools, etc., is the more important (I, 389-90; cf. V, 399b-400a). Nor does Jovellanos ever come to an unequivocal decision between his Neoclassic respect for art and his clear sentimental preference for nature.

III *Architectural Periods*

Jovellanos' view of historical periods in art reflects the evolution of his aesthetic thinking in the context of his fundamental and permanent Classical bias. For our author, Greek architecture is the *nec plus ultra* of taste, even after he has learned to appreciate the Gothic; and Roman architecture is only a corruption of the Greek (I, 351, 377a, n. 6; V, 377a). Moorish architecture, which lies outside the Classical-Renaissance-Neoclassic mainstream, is largely ignored. In the 1780's Jovellanos praises the elegance of the Moorish buildings of Cordova, Granada, and Seville (I, 364-65; II, 287a); yet his account of the development "of the fine arts in Spain from their origin to their present state" mentions, of all the Moorish monuments, only the Alhambra, and that in passing (I, 354b).

The Classical bias of Jovellanos also shows in his dislike for heavy ornamentation. Hence comments such as "Its architecture is Plateresque, but graceful," a grudging concession which implies the essential gracelessness of this charming style (D II, 85; cf. I, 386b, n. 12). No wonder, then, that the Baroque architect Churriguera is deemed a "heresiarch of good taste" (II, 288a). Jovellanos, like many of his contemporaries, considers the Baroque a corruption of all the arts, a contagion of affectation and triviality that entered Spain from Italy (I, 357b-58a, 372a, 387a, n. 13). (Italians, of course, claimed that the corruption originated in Spain.) Conversely, Jovellanos admires the grandiosely severe: the "marvel" of the Escorial (I, 353a; IV, 251b) and the architecture of Christopher Wren, whose St. Paul's Cathedral he compares to the Roman St. Peter's (V, 371b).

Most interesting of Jovellanos' various judgments on historical periods, however, are his opinions on Gothic architecture, the appreciation of which was to play a large role in the rise of Romanticism. In 1781 Jovellanos explains the Gothic style as a Germanic imitation of Byzantine architecture. He finds it defective and artless, that is, not adjusted to the Neoclassic rules of proportion; yet he discerns a crude but interesting cultural rebirth in the thirteenth century, especially in church architecture: "The minds of those artists seem to have devoted all their knowledge to inventing a dwelling worthy of the Supreme Being. When man enters one of those temples, he feels himself penetrated by a deep and silent reverence, which captures his spirit and gently leads it to the contemplation of the eternal truths" (I, 351). In 1795, at the sight of the Cathedral of León, Jovellanos exclaims: "What a beautiful, magnificent, sublime temple!" (D II, 28). The religious awe produced by medieval, and particularly Gothic, churches, impressed Catholic and conservative Romantics in the style of Chateaubriand, and texts similar to those quoted abound in the early nineteenth century. Nevertheless, Jovellanos' Neoclassic eye contradicts his Pre-Romantic heart and continues to find the Gothic cathedrals overloaded with useless detail and ornament, and devoid of proper proportions.

In 1786 Jovellanos puts forward the conjecture, formed, according to him, "long ago," that Gothic architecture descends from the Arab (I, 368a), which, in turn, he had earlier deemed an imitation of Byzantine architecture (I, 351b; cf. II, 286b-87a). The most extensive treatment of this question is found in the *Eulogy of Ventura Rodríguez* (I, 371b, and 378b-86, nn. 9-11). Here Jovellanos speaks of the "corruption" of ancient architecture at the hands of Persians, Arabs, and Byzantines. The result is Gothic architecture, which, according to our author, appears in Europe suddenly and in full perfection at the time of the crusades. Working with an imprecise chronology and failing to see the transition from the Romanesque style to the Gothic, Jovellanos links the elements of the latter to the architecture found by the crusaders in the Near East and to their own military constructions. He stresses the harmony between the characteristics of this architecture and those of the age that produced it, martial, gallant, and superstitious. He recognizes in the Gothic style a striving for daring, delicacy, and profusion; but he also sees in it an example of the aberrations of genius when inspired only by *capricho*, that is, unguided by the reason which for the Neoclassicist is essential to art and without which the mind produces only monsters, as Goya shows in one of those etchings entitled, precisely, *Caprichos.*

In his account of Gothic architecture, Jovellanos also recognizes the historical value of "Asturian architecture," the Pre-Romanesque monuments like San Miguel de Lillo and Santa María de Naranco, outside Oviedo. Although the "Arabic" traces which he sees in them may actually be remnants of the Visigothic style, copied by, not derived from, the Arabs, Jovellanos senses the influences which underlie the later *mudéjar* architecture, built by Moorish artisans for Christian masters.

During his imprisonment on Majorca, Jovellanos still maintains the theory of the origins of the Gothic style which he had developed in the *Eulogy of Ventura Rodríguez* (V, 375 ff.). He still finds it difficult to approve completely of this style, but he is increasingly attracted and impressed by it. Thus he finds that the cathedral of Palma, "without being beautiful or elegant, has about it something great and majestic which surprises and particularly delights the eye" (V, 361a). In the *lonja* he recognizes a "great and strange" beauty (V, 363b). The contemplation of the castle of Bellver leads him to evoke animated scenes of siege, defense, and peaceful festivities in its halls. At sunset, Bellver recalls an enchanted castle from the heroic fantasies of Ariosto (I, 395, 398b-99a). These and similar appreciations show a continued reluctance to credit the medieval buildings with those qualities (beauty, elegance) which, for the Neoclassicist, are inseparable from reason, order, and restraint, along with an increasing recognition of those qualities more linked to emotion (grandeur, majesty, "strange" beauty). Thus Jovellanos came to abandon the opinion, sometimes expressed also by him, that the Middle Ages were a time only of darkness (I, 319a). He came to appreciate the Christian and chivalric ideals of that epoch, which Romanticism was to exploit as literary themes.

Jovellanos must have approved of the anti-Baroque trend in the architecture of his own time but, strangely enough, he has left us little testimony of his interest in his contemporaries in this field, other than Ventura Rodríguez. On the other hand, many diary entries and more extensive writings witness to his lasting and lively concern with the architecture of the past and the conservation and comprehension of its monuments.

IV *Painting*

Jovellanos approached painting with the same principles that governed his view of architecture. Thus he found medieval paintings, beginning with the thirteenth century, occasionally pleasing; but, as we have seen, he missed in them that exact proportion which, in his opinion, can alone yield a satisfying harmony (I, 351b-52a). He hailed Michelangelo as the "main restorer" of the arts, studied and surpassed by Raphael (I, 352a, 370).

Among the Spanish masters of the sixteenth and seventeenth centuries, Jovellanos appreciates Zurbarán (I, 354a) but reserves his most fervent admiration for Velázquez and Murillo. He praises Velázquez' technique, his faithful imitation of models taken from nature, and his ability to create illusion, perhaps in such works as *The Spinners* and *The Meninas* (I, 356). And enthusiastically he exclaims: "How can I omit Murillo, the gentle and delicate Murillo, whose skillful brush gave to canvas all the charms of beauty and of gracefulness? Oh great Murillo! In your works I have believed the miracles of art and talent; I have seen the atmosphere, the atoms, the air, the dust, the movement of the waters, and even the tremulous glow of the morning light painted in them" (I, 354a).

As is to be expected, Jovellanos has little use for El Greco, the very model of an "idealistic" rather than a "naturalistic" painter. He credits him with stimulating the arts and with defending the dignity of painting as an art, not a trade; but he finds his style "dry" and "disagreeable" and is repelled by what he considers the Cretan's extravagances (I, 332b, 353, 357a, 358a).

Jovellanos befriended his contemporary Goya, admiring his "skillful and vigorous brush" (I, 388b, n. 16); and Goya is the author of the best-known portrait of Jovellanos, one which shows him seated at a table, resting his head on his hand in a somewhat melancholy pose.[2] Like all of his age, Jovellanos pays tribute to the eighteenth-century painter and aesthetic theorist Anton Rafael Mengs. Born in Aussig an der Elbe (or Ústí nad Labem) in Bohemia, Mengs came to be the court painter of Charles III of Spain; and a sizeable collection of his work can be seen in the Prado Museum in Madrid and in several royal palaces in and around the Spanish capital. Although now almost forgotten, Mengs had enormous influence and prestige in the eighteenth century, and particularly in Spain. Jovellanos, who in principle rejected "idealism" in art and favored the "naturalism" of Velázquez, nevertheless eulogized the genius of the "idealist" Mengs a few years after his death, calling him "a gigantic artist, rising above and dazzling the rest, . . . the son of Apollo and Minerva, the philosopher-painter, the master, the benefactor and lawgiver of the arts." Not only are Mengs's paintings, according to Jovellanos, "divine," but his writings are "the catechism of good taste."[3]

Over the years Jovellanos formed a valuable collection of drawings and preliminary sketches by numerous well-known painters. This testimony to his artistic taste, priceless for the student of painting, was stored, along with Jovellanos' papers, in the Royal Asturian Institute in Gijón; and, having been transferred, along with them, to the building that also housed the Simancas Barracks, it was destroyed in the Republican bombardment of that Nationalist stronghold at the outbreak of the Spanish Civil War in 1936. While on Majorca, Jovellanos gave detailed advice and criticism to the painter Fray Manuel Bayeu (II, 155 ff.), showing considerable detailed knowledge of the art and craft of painting. After his return to the mainland he spent some time in the house of his friend Juan Arias de Saavedra in Jadraque (Province of Guadalajara). There one can still see a room decorated with frescoes which are said to be the work of Jovellanos. These paintings, not devoid of charm but, on the whole, lacking outstanding artistic merit, must have some connection with Don Gaspar's stay, since his intervention would best explain the fact that one of them depicts the castle of Bellver; but in view of the absolute silence of Jovellanos' diary, in general so detailed, with respect to any activity of this kind, at this time of his life or any other, I doubt that his hand was the sole or even principal one.[4]

V   *Literature in General*

Jovellanos' critical and theoretical opinions about literature are to some extent implicit in his creative work, which we have already examined; but they are also explicit in letters, diary, discourses, and pedagogical writings.

The basis of Jovellanos' view of literature is Neoclassical, Horatian. Our author would have students memorize Horace's *Art of Poetry* and his first epistle of Book II, "for they suffice to form a kind of code of good taste."[5] The *Course in Spanish Humanities*, derived from Hugh Blair's *Lectures on Rhetoric and Belles Lettres* and of suspect authorship (Caso, *Poesías*, p. 17, n. 1), nevertheless reflects the outlines of Jovellanos' views, even if not the details of wording. It adheres firmly to the Horatian principle of *utile dulci* as the dual justification of literature: to please and move the reader or spectator is the principal or immediate aim of the literary work of art, while useful instruction is the secondary, indirect, or ultimate aim (I, 137b, 142a). Precision and clarity are the stylistic ideals; literary language should be "like a clear river, where one can see as far as the bottom" (I, 114a). In other words, the language should not itself attract attention, as occurs in Baroque poetry and prose; it should faithfully convey the author's thought, the beauty of the work consisting more of the scenes and actions described than of the language used to describe them.

In Pre-Romantic fashion, the *Course* concerns itself with the sublime and finds it particularly in the mysterious. The sublime, we read, is not only the large or the high, but also the roar of wind or thunder and the flash of lightning. "Among the great and sublime objects [we must include] the frightful noise of waters plunging from a great height, a very dense darkness, the deep silence of a forest or a lonely countryside, the majestic sound of a great bell, especially in the midst of the silence or calm of the night, and, in general, many nocturnal scenes . . ." (I, 128b). In this respect the *Course* reflects what Jovellanos had already practiced in the "Epistle from Fabio to Anfriso."

As Professor Russell P. Sebold has made clear, by "imitation" the Neoclassicists did not understand simple copying, but rather an author's accepting an inspiration and trying to follow it and even to beat it at its own game.[6] It is in this sense that Vergil imitated Homer, who was for him both a model and a rival to be outdone. In 1793 Jovellanos challenges this doctrine, though, since his considerations are addressed to the author of a deplorable imitation of *Don Quixote,* they may above all be an attempt to soften the blow of Jovellanos' negative reaction. Jovellanos claims that imitation limits the imagination, and that imitation of great models, in which failure is so easy and so obvious, is especially dangerous. Even a mediocre degree of originality is to be prized more highly than imitation (IV, 183, 186b).

In another break with strict Neoclassicism, which demands careful separation of genres and of the different arts, Jovellanos, while on Majorca, expresses his admiration for English descriptive literature. The English, he believes, have successfully com-

bined the study of the fine arts and literature; and their writings
are consequently filled with descriptions of objects and actions
that charm and move the heart (V, 379b). Jovellanos values the
sentimental success of this literature above formal perfection or
adherence to Neoclassic rules.

A few years later, however, Jovellanos writes that the purpose
of poetry is "to please and instruct by means of figurative language subjected to measure and harmony, and embellished with
fictions and agreeable descriptions" (I, 270a). His concept of
literature remains basically Neoclassic, though at various times
he emphasizes his appreciation of sentiment, originality, and
other factors which were to become essentials of the subsequent
Romantic creed.

VI *Poetry*

Jovellanos believes that poetry must steer between the vicious
extremes of prosaicism and bombast. He sees prosaicism as the
flaw of an overly rational poetry. The poet must use imagination more than reason in order to create a graphic language. In
other words, poetry must speak primarily to the senses, as it
does in Jovellanos' own more successful poems. Bombast, on
the other hand, results from excessive reliance on the imagination in disregard of the musical qualities of poetry, essential
for Jovellanos (I, 247a).

Poetry seeks to please and artfully to arrange the inventions
of the imagination, but these essential aims can also be accom-
plished by prose. Jovellanos therefore accepts the existence of
poetic prose, relegating meter to the status of a secondary characteristic of poetry (I, 137b-38a, 247b). Furthermore, both
poetry and verse are to be differentiated from rhyme. Although
rhyme "unquestionably adds great beauty to poetry," Jovellanos
finds it difficult to adapt his ideas to its demands (II, 315b; D
II, 148; cf. I, 140b). His best poems are all written in blank hendecasyllables.

Jovellanos values epic and didactic poetry above the lyrical
and, especially, the erotic; but he finds these genres appropriate
enough for youth and grants them the merit of serving as practice for higher forms (II, 273a; Caso, *Poesías*, pp. 90, 117 ff.).

Although he did not himself make the "laws" and discoveries of natural science the subject of his verses, as did other poets of the eighteenth and early nineteenth centuries, his prose on occasion shows his appreciation of the poetic qualities of science (I, 339b-40a).

In 1773, Jovellanos recommends a number of authorities for the study of poetics, including Aristotle, Horace, and Jouvancy, a French Jesuit whose work is "the best thing I have read" (II, 167a). Luzán is strikingly absent from this list; but after his *Poetics* was reedited in 1789, he holds an important place among Jovellanos' authorities, especially as a guide to models of good writing (*Calatrava*, p. 144; I, 246b-47a). Like Luzán and most of his own contemporaries, Jovellanos believes that Spanish poetry reached its high point in the sixteenth century, under the influence of the Classics and the Italians of the Renaissance, themselves heavily influenced by the Classics. In that age flourished most of the poets whom Jovellanos especially recommends: Garcilaso de la Vega, Herrera, Rioja, Ercilla, Balbuena, the Argensolas, "and above all, Fray Luis de León himself." From earlier periods, Jovellanos appreciates Juan de Mena and Jorge Manrique. After the zenith of the sixteenth century, poets ceased to exercise the necessary restraints; and their unbridled imaginations led to the corruption of taste which Jovellanos finds in the verses of Lope de Vega and Góngora. Still, he does not condemn all the works of these poets; Góngora was read in the Royal Asturian Institute, probably in his ballads, which throughout the Neoclassic period stood as an example of what the great Baroque poet could achieve when he resisted the aesthetic current of his time. In the latter eighteenth century Jovellanos finds signs of a poetic renovation which makes him optimistic about the future. This becomes plain in the *Theoretical-Practical Treatise on Education*, where Meléndez, Leandro F. de Moratín, and the young poets Cienfuegos and Quintana are placed in the category of Homer, Horace, Vergil, Milton, and Racine (I, 247b; D II, 315; *Calatrava*, p. 137; Caso, *Poesías*, pp. 92-94).

VII *Drama*

Jovellanos considered the drama potentially superior to the

other arts because it combines several of them, and of great moral importance because of its direct access to a mass public (I, 226a, 495). Ideally, the theater should inculcate principles of religion, citizenship, family obligations, and friendship; and in order to make sure that it does, it must be controlled by the state, either directly or through especially created academies (I, 496a, 498b-99a).

According to Jovellanos, who, except in *The Honest Culprit*, remained faithful to Neoclassic dramatic standards, "Lope [de Vega] filled our theaters with irregular and monstrous plays which banished order, truth, and decorum from the stage" (I, 358b). Lope "finally brought comedy to that point of artifice and ostentation in which ignorance saw the height of its perfection, and sound criticism, the seeds of the depravation and ruin of our stage" (I, 489b). The works of Calderón de la Barca and Moreto, like those of other playwrights of the Golden Age, are similarly defective when judged by Neoclassic standards; yet Jovellanos believed that they would continue to please the public. He condemns the religious allegorical *autos sacramentales*, prohibited by the government of Charles III, as full of foolish and indecent matter contrary to their supposed edifying aims. Jovellanos' judgment on the plays of his own day is not much more favorable. Unlike some of the other arts, drama does not seem to him to be progressing (I, 488-90).

VIII *Prose*

The prose writers whom Jovellanos admires belong, like his model poets, to the sixteenth and early seventeenth centuries. Among others, they include the historian Juan de Mariana, the religious authors Fray Luis de Granada and Fray Luis de León (previously cited as a poet), and Cervantes (*Calatrava*, p. 137; D I, 453). Neoclassic literary theorists usually ignored prose fiction, which was considered little more than artless ramblings of the fantasy. Something like this view underlies Torcuato's exclamation in *The Honorable Culprit* (I, 99b): "Everything that is happening seems like a novel (*novela*); I am stunned and hardly believe what I see with my own eyes." *Novela* here suggests an extravagant tale, as it still did as late as the mid-nineteenth century. Jovellanos explains that this genre originally sought only to amuse, thus falling short of the dual aim of literature as Neoclassicism understood it. A new and more dangerous element, however, a new morality, is to be found in modern French productions. The potentially sound moral influence of the novel is shown by the examples of Samuel Richàrdson and other English authors; but their works also must be purged of passages offensive to Spanish political and moral tenets (II, 535b-36a).

Like most critics of the eighteenth century, Jovellanos considers *Don Quixote* as primarily a satire of chivalric ideas (I, 485b). He criticizes Cervantes for setting his tale in his own time, which, in Jovellanos' opinion, destroys its verisimilitude. Like Neoclassic tragedy, fiction, in order to be credible, must be removed from the reader's everyday world either in time (the historical fiction to be cultivated later by the Romantics) or in space, like the Renaissance epics of Ercilla and Camões (IV, 183b-84b).

IX   *Nature and Landscape*

No discussion of Jovellanos' artistic and aesthetic ideas would be complete without some attention to his appreciation of landscapes and of nature in general. Our author was sensitive to natural scenes and expressed this sensitivity not only in his lyrics, but also in his diary, which records his impressions while in Gijón and on Majorca and while traveling through central and northern Spain.

Jovellanos loved the mountains of his native Asturias, its coast, and its green, intensively cultivated, humanized countryside. Unlike many other Spaniards, even of this day, he had a special fondness for trees, which he planted and lovingly observed (D II, 134, 304 *et passim*). They are important in landscape descriptions like this one, reminiscent of a twentieth-century poem by Jorge Guillén: "Departure from Valladolid at a quarter past seven. The road follows the cattle path; the Pisuerga [river] on the right; leafy banks, on which white poplars grow" (D I, 219; see also D II, 112-13). An old tree is compared to a patriarch surrounded by the family he has sired (V, 351). The shade of a tree which, with a nearby brook, tempers the heat of the day, and a similar scene by moonlight, impress Jovellanos with their poetry (D I, 283; D II, 73-74).

In general, Jovellanos preferred the intimate scenes of nature, discreetly limited, fruitful and therefore useful to man. This tendency is clear in the Majorcan writings (V, 345 ff.), describing the picturesque contrast between the rugged mountains and the plain, where all is "renewed and beautified by the industry of man." After sketching bucolic scenes interspersed with monasteries and funereal cypresses, our author returns to his ideal of an ordered variety. Neatly planted mulberry trees combine utility and beauty in their symmetry, but tedious uniformity is avoided by the fact that the pattern of trees differs from one field to the next. "And since their various shapes and colors also contrast in that skillful way that only the wise hand of nature can find, far from giving the scene that air of artificiality and deliberate regularity that is so tiresome in our city parks, they shed over it the most pleasing harmony." One notes the preference for the ease of nature over the constraint of the formal garden, but also Jovellanos' enduring utilitarianism. The Bay of Palma is likewise calm and useful; utility, contrast, and variety within regularity are the watchwords of Jovellanos' description of it. Nature, for him, is imperfect without man: "But what is spring, and what would all of nature be, if, still and lonely, she neither heard the voice nor felt the hand of man, whose task it is to train and guide her? . . . Thus, in this scene, the presence of man and his dwelling and his constant labors give the crowning touch to all this beauty" (V, 349a).

Jovellanos could also feel the attraction of the valley of Covadonga, set among the craggy mountains of Asturias, and of other wild and sublime scenes (I, 373b-74a; IV, 146b; D I, 334). The following is a seascape observed from a hill near his house in Gijón:

I cannot dismiss from my memory the situation of Santa Catalina last night. The dubious and mournful light of the sky; the vastness of the sea, revealed from time to time by frightful lightning that shattered the distant horizon; the dull noise of the waters breaking among the rocks at the foot of the hill; the solitude, the calmness, and the silence of all living beings made the scene sublime and magnificent beyond words. In the midst of it, my meditations were interrupted by the "Who goes there?" of a sentinel posted in a doorway of the chapel, who, upon hearing my reply, began to sing in the mournful mode of the region; and this solitary voice, from which I gradually drew farther away, contrasted marvellously with the universal silence. Man, if you wish to be happy, contemplate Nature and draw near her; in her is the source of that little pleasure and felicity that were granted to your being. (D I, 467-468)

The harsher landscapes of Castile, so dear to the Generation of 1898, found no favorable echo in Jovellanos' sensibility. Castile, for him, was an "arid country, disagreeable, without wood, without pleasing fruits, without population" (D I, 119). He did not find in it his beloved trees, nor the symbiosis of land and man.

We have seen how Jovellanos found a harmony between his subjective state and the landscape of El Paular; and on Majorca, too, he discovers kinship between a shaded solitude and the "gentle melancholy of [his] soul" (V, 351a). The contemplation of landscape can also stimulate Jovellanos' imagination to recreate scenes of the past. Thus the description of a Roman road leads to an evocation of the Roman troops that had used it; and Majorcan scenes recall the battles of the conquest of that island—the shouts, the neighing, the banners, and the clash of arms (V, 353b).

Jovellanos' appreciation of nature was the inspiration of some of his best verses, as well as a source of comfort and happiness throughout his life. Both in nature and in art, Jovellanos had, for his time, considerable understanding for the extravagant; but in the last analysis he adhered always to an initial predilection for order, symmetry, and utility. In this, as in so many other things, he was a true son of the Enlightenment. Both art and nature were, for him, part of a harmonious world and, in the case of nature, a link between man and God.

CHAPTER 5

Economics

I   *Jovellanos' Introduction to Economics*

JOVELLANOS' interest in economics developed during his ten years in Seville and lasted throughout his lifetime, although in later years partially submerged in educational and political concerns. Economics, education, and politics were for him closely allied fields; the power of the modern state, he believed, depends to a large extent on its wealth (II, 38b), while the distribution of wealth within society affects the position of the social classes. Economics is, then, the science of government *par excellence*, the key to increased individual welfare and national prosperity (I, 313-15). This concept of economic science is analogous to that which Jovellanos' age held of the natural sciences: in economics, as in physics, certain "natural forces" and "laws" were to be discovered. Man could not change these laws, but he could benefit from them by adapting himself to them.

Although economics was ignored by the universities of his time, which continued to stress juridical and theological training, Jovellanos found in the Seville of Olavide a propitious climate for such study. Olavide himself was busy with economic questions, especially as superintendent of the ambitious development project in the Sierra Morena; and in his circle, the latest foreign and domestic books were read and discussed. In Seville Jovellanos must have first read the economic treatises of Richard Cantillon and Condillac, whom, until the mid-1780's, he considered the foremost authorities on the subject (II, 440). From then on, his economic thinking was increasingly influenced by English authors, particularly by Adam Smith. Jovellanos' familiarity with the principal Spanish economic writers must also date from the Seville period. The main works of Campomanes were published during this time, and we know from Jovellanos' correspondence with that author that he had read at least one of them before leaving for Madrid (II, 139). When an Economic Society was founded in Seville in 1775, Jovellanos was one of its first members (Ceán, p. 133); and both in this capacity and as a magistrate, he found himself engaged in economic studies and the preparation of reports on economic subjects.

II *The Economic Situation of Spain*

The agrarian question occupied Spanish economists and politicians throughout the eighteenth century. In the midst of arguments about whether or not Spanish agriculture was in decline, there was a constant desire to expand production and to reduce the concentration of land ownership. Toward the middle of the century, the king, the nobles, and the Church held about four-fifths of all land; toward the end of the century the nobles and clergy, constituting about one twentieth of the population, owned some two-thirds of all arable land.[1] This situation created economic, political, and religious problems which the government attempted, with only partial success, to solve.

The state also sought to promote industrialization by establishing factories as "pilot projects," protecting nascent industries, encouraging the immigration of foreign artisans and technicians, and fostering the dissemination of scientific and technical information. The period as a whole was one of falling real wages, and the consequent profit inflation spurred industrial development while depressing the lot of the urban worker.[2] The declining guild system, condemned by economists of all schools and no longer favored by government, was unable to stop this trend. Commerce, in Spain as in other countries, was frequently hampered by restrictions. Some of these stemmed from a fear of scarcity of such vital products as grain; others reflected a mercantilist "fear of goods" and consequent desire to force exports and restrict imports. Some theorists considered trade economically unproductive and thought it would be socially useful to "eliminate the middleman." Others concentrated their attention on foreign trade, from which, through export surpluses, they hoped to obtain precious metals and thus assure the health and strength of the State. They believed that such exports supported the population at the expense of foreigners. These and other problems are dealt with in Jovellanos' economic writings.

III   *Jovellanos'* Report on the Agrarian Law

The outstanding expression of Jovellanos' economic principles is the *Informe en el expediente de ley agraria (Report on the Agrarian Law)* of 1795. Complaints, analyses, and suggested remedies concerning Spain's agrarian problem had found their way to the Council of Castile, the supreme governing body, which, at the suggestion of its counsel Campomanes, entrusted the *expediente* or dossier relating to agrarian reform to the Economic Society of Madrid, of which Campomanes was director. In order to aid the Society in the task of preparing a report and suggesting policy, an abstract of the various writings was printed in 1784; and by January of the following year the agricultural committee of the Society was at work on the project. Progress, however, was slow. In 1787 Jovellanos, one of the members of the committee, was asked to formulate a plan for a report; and the following year he was charged with writing the report. Each member of the committee submitted his views on the causes of the decadence of agriculture in Spain; and Jovellanos accepted, reconciled, or rejected the widely-differing opinions.[3] His report, though reflecting its preparation in the name of the Economic Society, was the work of Jovellanos alone. He did not submit it to the Society until April of 1794, after his "exile" in Gijón had given him additional leisure to work on it; and it was enthusiastically received by the Society, which published it the following year.

The economic principle on which Jovellanos bases his report is self-interest. Although laws must contain its excesses and constrain it within the bounds of justice, their chief aim must be to remove the impediments to self-interest, which normally is self-regulating and which, when functioning properly, is the surest way to individual and collective well-being. Jovellanos distinguishes three classes of impediments to this proper functioning. The first and most important are obstacles created by legislation, and Jovellanos suggests remedies for them. Communally owned lands should be given over to private ownership and development. The laws prohibiting enclosure and otherwise limiting property rights to favor sheep raisers at the expense of agriculture should be repealed, so that farmers will improve cultivation in the assurance that wandering herds will not destroy their crops. In this way Jovellanos expects also to encourage settlement of farmers on the land, instead of their living in a village and cultivating distant fields. The benefits of such resettlement are not only economic:

An immense rural population spread out among the fields promises the state a people not only hard-working and rich, but also simple and virtuous. The tenant, living on his plot and free from the clash of the passions which agitate men when they are gathered in towns, will be farther removed from that ferment of corruption which, more or less actively, luxury always infuses in them. Gathered with his family in the scene of his labor, he can, on the one hand, pursue the only object of his interest without distraction, and, on the other, he will feel more forcefully drawn to it by the sentiments of love and tenderness natural to man in domestic society. Then we shall not only be able to expect from our farmers diligence, frugality, and the abundance born of these two, but conjugal, paternal, filial, and fraternal love will reign in their families; peace, charity, and hospitality will reign, and our tenants will possess those social and domestic virtues which make for the happiness of families and the true glory of states. (II, 90a)

Although he recognized that certain terrains and climates are more suitable for large-scale exploitation, Jovellanos cherished the ideal of the small self-sufficient farmer living close to the soil in virtuous simplicity and moderate well-being. What for many was a poetic theme was for him also an important consideration in economic policy.

The accumulation of property, the goal and result of the operation of self-interest, produces an undesirable inequality among men; but Jovellanos seeks the remedy for this evil in its cause: the desire of others to accumulate property, if allowed to exercise itself, will always redistribute property and thus prevent permanent gross inequalities (II, 98b). The law, however, interferes with this remedy by providing for cases in which property, once acquired, can never be sold. The concentration of ownership is thus progressive and irreversible. Negotiable land becomes scarcer and therefore more expensive. Although land ownership continues to bring prestige and is therefore desired, yields on capital thus invested fall, and improvements are discouraged. The number of landowners decreases and the proportion of tenants, already very high in some provinces, rises.

All of these are evils in Jovellanos' view, and he proceeds to attack them. He declares mortmain, the inalienable possession by ecclesiastical bodies, to be illegal in origin, even though subsequently sanctioned by legislation; and he blames the accumulation of land by the Church for the decline of Castile: "What has remained of that former glory but the skeletons of her cities, once populous and full of factories and workshops, of warehouses and stores, and today inhabited only by churches, convents, and hospitals, which survive the wretchedness they have caused?" (II, 100b). Jovellanos asks that further passage of land into mortmain be prohibited and that the clergy be encouraged voluntarily to dispose of their lands through sale or long-term leases.

Civil entails were even more widespread than mortmain, and Jovellanos considers them equally pernicious. The creator of a *mayorazgo* or entail in primogeniture, could establish the inalienability of his property for all time, perpetually favoring the eldest sons of his family and beggaring all other descendants. Jovellanos considers this system contrary to the laws of reason and nature. Property is, in his opinion, a natural right derived from man's right to his body and the labor of that body; but the right to transmit property by will is established not by natural but by positive law and therefore modifiable by it (II, 103b-4). Entails are not only unjust but socially harmful. Like mortmain, they restrict economic activity and accentuate inequality; and they increase the class of poor nobles who lack both the means to support their pretensions and the humility to acquire those means. The destitute and unproductive noble, useless to society, is a well-known figure in Spanish literature since the sixteenth-century picaresque novel *Lazarillo de Tormes.* Himself, however, a member of a noble family, Jovellanos understands that great wealth allows his class to play its role of disinterested service in the monarchic state (II, 105b, 291); and for this reason, and in recognition of the limits of the possible, he temporizes with entails, suggesting that some degree of alienation should be allowed and that further entail of land should only be permitted as a reward for very special merits.

Turning to other legal obstacles to the development of agriculture, Jovellanos condemns such restraints on trade as price controls. He believes that only competition can produce the cheapness and abundance which these measures seek to achieve. They reflect foolish prejudices against merchants and, while trying to limit or prevent their profits, interfere with the division of labor which for Jovellanos, as for Adam Smith, is one of the principal sources of wealth. Division of labor also applies to entire provinces; and to constrain trade between agricultural and industrial provinces is to reduce the productivity of both, since production will adjust itself to consumption. Many restraints were intended to prevent scarcity of grains or monopoly of grain supplies; but Jovellanos argues that such measures will, by restricting the market, produce the evils they seek to avoid (II, 108-13).

These arguments also apply, up to a point, to foreign trade. Jovellanos decries the mercantilistic policy of prohibiting exports of raw materials in order to force their elaboration at home and cheaply supply domestic industry. Such measures unfairly sacrifice agriculture to manufacturing and are furthermore self-defeating, since a restricted market will decrease production (*ibid*.). Only with respect to grain exports does Jovellanos depart from this line. Noting the vital necessity of grain and the importance of psychological factors in grain prices, he argues that the permission to export encourages fear of scarcity and high prices. Since, furthermore, there is as yet no proof of the existence of an exportable surplus, Jovellanos urges that export prohibitions be maintained at least provisionally (II, 114-17). Grain was, of course, the basic food of the masses of the people; and grain prices were thought to affect wages and, consequently, the price of manufactured goods. Any increase in grain prices, let alone a famine, was an evil to be avoided. This explains Jovellanos' deviation from his principles, though it does not strengthen his logic. Ultimately all prices are affected by psychological factors and by estimates of supply and demand (as opposed to the facts of supply and demand); and if restriction of the market depresses production of other items, including domestically-traded grain, the same should hold true with regard to foreign trade in grain. In fact, Jovellanos hesitated before he took his public position, which seems to owe something to the writings of the Swiss economist Jacques Necker; and he later disavowed privately what he had written in the name of the Economic Society.[4]

Jovellanos also urges reform of tax legislation. He argues that sales taxes in particular are regressive and hamper trade. They are offensive when levied on capital (e.g., land) whose product, when sold, will also be taxed; and they are particularly unfair because the wealthiest landowners, whose lands are amortized and thus cannot be sold, are exempt from them (II, 118b-19a).

The second class of obstacles to the development of agriculture includes erroneous opinions and ignorance. Although agriculture, Jovellanos maintains, is the chief source of prosperity and of moral and physical well-being, public policy has consistently neglected it in favor of commerce. The peasant, furthermore, has traditionally borne the main burden of taxes and personal services. To remedy these conditions Jovellanos urges the wider study of economics, in the belief that understanding will bring improvement. Outside the universities, from which, like other reformers, he expected little, Jovellanos wished to establish institutes in which the landowning classes could acquire practical knowledge that would help them to improve their management of the land. Peasants, with the assistance of the clergy and the Economic Societies, should also be educated, first to read and write, and then to improve their methods of cultivation by study of simple technical manuals (II, 124-26).

Natural obstacles to agricultural development constitute Jovellanos' third class and include lack of irrigation, of roads, of river and canal communications, and of improved seaports. Jovellanos urges the government to allot regularly to public works the money wasted on wars and useless ornamentation, proceeds from the sale of public lands, the labor of troops and local citizens, and the revenue from taxes (II, 132 ff.). Such taxes, Jovellanos declares, should be imposed on all citizens, and in proportion to their ability to pay—standards which seem modern enough until we note the author's preference for the salt tax, a perfectly regressive tax on consumption (II, 133a). In more general terms, Jovellanos asks that the quality of rural life be improved by decreasing useless and oppressive regimentation of the peasantry and allowing them to live more freely and more happily (II, 134b-35a).

The *Report on the Agrarian Law* was published in 1795 with the support of Godoy, whose government, hard pressed for revenues, hoped to impose new taxes on amortized lands (Herr, pp. 380 ff.). The Inquisition, however, also took notice of the work. Denunciation was followed by investigation, and the Inquisition's censors condemned Jovellanos' opinions on the property rights of the Church and saw dangerous egalitarian tendencies in his hostility toward entails. The inquisitorial process was ordered suspended in July, 1797, perhaps because of Jovellanos' rise in the favor of Godoy; and when Jovellanos began his ministry, he was entrusted with organizing the sale of the property of charitable institutions.[5] The years following the publication of the *Report* saw it translated into English, French, and German; and it has been repeatedly republished in Spain, notably in 1820, when a fuller and more accurate version than that of 1795 appeared. In 1812 the *cortes,* or parliament, recommended its study. Such marks of esteem, however, did not save the work from being placed on the *Index of Forbidden Books* in 1825 and remaining there for a hundred years. Many of Jovellanos' proposals were not put into practice until the nineteenth century.

IV *Property*

The foundations of Jovellanos' economics are three interrelated principles: private property rights, self-interest, and liberty. Like St. Thomas Aquinas and the Irish philosopher Francis Hutcheson, whom he admired and who was Adam Smith's teacher, Jovellanos conceives of property rights as grounded in natural law but modified by society.[6] Justified by their social usefulness, their exercise can be regulated by society in order to further this aim. Jovellanos here occupies the middle ground between those who, like Locke, Smith, and Condillac, see property as a natural right independent of society and one which governments are instituted to safeguard, and those who would derive all property rights from the State. The latter group includes Grotius, Hobbes, Montesquieu, and Rousseau. For Jovellanos, as for Adam Smith, property rights originate in every man's right to the labor of his own body; the sanctity of this labor sanctifies the fruits of labor and establishes man's most basic property right, the right to work.[7]

Jovellanos deals with this topic most explicitly in his *Informe sobre el libre ejercicio de las artes* (*Report on the Free Exercise of Crafts*), 1785, II, 33-45, where, like most economists of his time, he attacks labor guilds. It was alleged that restrictive guild practices raised wages and therefore prices—an argument which, at least for Spain, is belied by the sharp decline in real wages (about 20% increase of money wages, as against a doubling of prices) in the second half of the eighteenth century (Hamilton, pp. 208, 214, 215, 220). Jovellanos, like Campomanes, also favored the development of cottage industries and accused the guilds of concentrating manufactures in the large cities. He further believed that they resisted innovation and the division of labor. Finally, guilds, by interfering with free contracts between employee and employer, restricted the former's rights in his labor.

Jovellanos' proposals—the abolition of guilds and their replacement with government-sponsored craft registers and advisers from the Economic Societies—draw heavily on Campomanes.[8] In effect, they replace guild controls with governmental controls, eliminating a pocket of autonomy unwelcome to the centralism of Enlightened Despotism; but the freedom and welfare of the laborer are not necessarily advanced by this change. Furthermore, the freedom of contract between employee and employer depends on equality between the contracting parties. Jovellanos and his contemporaries, in all good faith, failed to recognize the bargaining advantage which the abolition of guilds would give to employers. The fall of real wages shows that the decline of the guilds was accompanied by a lowering of labor's standard of living, even though employment may also have become more widespread.

V *Self-Interest*

Property is important to Jovellanos because he believes, like Adam Smith, that the desire to acquire it, that is, the "pursuit of happiness," if freely exercised within the bounds of justice, is the surest way to the prosperity of the individual; and since society consists of individuals, collective prosperity will be augmented as individuals flourish (I, 264b; II, 88; IV, 230-32). He explains that an enlightened government will recognize that in their self-interest men have a sufficiently powerful stimulus to seek their private well-being, and it will allow this self-interest to act freely. It will recognize that the public interest is inseparable from this individual interest, and therefore it will not trouble to promote the former by directing the latter. It will be vigilant, but not uneasy; and in place of this constant pressure and flux of laws and regulations, which instead of stimulating and guiding the operation of self-interest only hinder and discourage it, it will bestow on it only that watchful but passive protection which moves to check self-interest when it breaks the bounds of justice. (IV, 198a)

This faith in the operation of self-interest was shared by most of the economists of Jovellanos' time, although they differed on whether this principle was powerful enough to overcome obstacles unaided, and whether its goodness was absolute. Adam Smith and Jovellanos both believed that no law can be more effective than a man's own interest in directing his economic activities toward his own welfare, and they therefore distrust both stimuli and impediments to this interest. This does not, however, mean that they favor untrammeled self-interest, since both recognize the existence of a public interest and of norms of justice which may need protection.[9] Both are concerned with the welfare of the individual, and particularly of the worker. "No society," writes Adam Smith, "can surely be flourishing and happy, of which the far greater part of the members are poor and miserable. It is but equity, besides, that they who feed, cloath and lodge the whole body of the people, should have such a share of the produce of their own labour as to be themselves tolerably well fed, cloathed and lodged" (p. 79). Jovellanos similarly writes to Antonio Ponz:

I see, my friend, that there is much talk of public welfare and little of individual welfare; that we seek more peasants, and not food and clothing for these peasants; that we want many artisans and craftsmen, and that they should be content with a wretched wage. These ideas seem to me somewhat bizarre. They place the people, that is, the class which is most necessary and most worthy of care, in a miserable condition; they found the opulence of the rich on the misery of the poor and base the well-being of the State on the oppression of the members of that very State. (II, 294)

Shortly after the publication of the *Report on the Agrarian Law*, Jovellanos declares: "I . . . shall recognize no public prosperity that is not derived from and based on individual prosperity; and all talk of national power, riches, glory, and well-being will seem to me vain and dismal unless it represents individual portions of the goods to which we apply these names."[10]

By way of contrast, mercantilists, much of whose thinking survives in such contemporaries of Jovellanos' as Campomanes, were primarily interested in strengthening the relative position of the State in the political competition with other States; and they normally considered the welfare of the individual only as a means to the ends of the State. How else can one explain their ideal of a low-wage economy producing abundant goods which are then exchanged for the silver and gold of foreigners?

Does self-interest produce the results which Jovellanos and others expected from it? Jovellanos overestimated the ease with which the factors of production can shift from one line of endeavor to another, and perhaps he failed to distinguish adequately between short-run interest and long-term interest. He recognized that for its perfect operation, self-interest should be perfectly enlightened, and that this was not the case; hence his insistence on the importance of education as an adjunct to economic development. And while he believed that even with these impediments the free exercise of self-interest, in the form of free competition, is its own best regulator, he occasionally called for legal interference with its operation. Thus he favored prohibiting the excessive subdivision of farms in his native Asturias, explaining that as long as law directed and controlled economic activity in general, it ought also to prevent farmers from creating, with the best of intentions, holdings so small as not to be viable (II, 291-93).

VI   *Liberty*

Jovellanos summed up his ideal economic program as *libertad, luces y auxilios* ("liberty, enlightenment, and assistance") II, 69b, 74b. By the last, he meant such public works as roads, ports, and canals. By *luces* he meant the education of all classes so that each individual might be able to discern his own true interest and be aided in pursuing it effectively. By liberty, Jovellanos meant that capital should be able to move without hindrance from one investment to another and be freely exploited, without such restraints as entail, prohibition of enclosure, etc.; that labor should be able to contract freely with em-

ployers for its services, without the restrictions of the guild system; and that trade should be free from oppressive taxation and
from prohibitions and price controls. As early as 1774, and repeatedly thereafter, he argues that only freely determined market prices are just and that efforts to fix a "fair price" by law
are necessarily either pointless (if they coincide with the market
price) or unjust (if they violate the principle of liberty and force
prices either up or down) II, 2-3, 53, 108-10, 473; V, 223b.
Furthermore, artificially low prices, designed to insure a cheap
and plentiful supply, will have results contrary to those intended: by depressing profits, they will curtail production. With regard to foreign trade, Jovellanos, while free of the mercantilists'
obsession with a "favorable" balance of trade, vacillates between
arguments for free trade and a moderately protectionist policy
designed to encourage developing industries (II, 50-52, 72; V,
225a).

VII   *Wealth, Money, and Prices*

In spite of occasional lapses, Jovellanos normally thinks of
national wealth in terms of goods, with money being only a sign
of value, not a value in itself (II, 443a). His economic proposals
are therefore oriented toward increasing the domestic consumption of goods—in other words, the material well-being of the
population—rather than toward the export surpluses dear to
mercantilists. He likewise differs with mercantilism in his assess-
ment of the role of commerce and manufactures. For Jovellanos,
the most fruitful source of wealth is agriculture, in which the
spontaneous productivity of nature is joined to that of labor
and capital and which, through abundance of raw materials and
cheapness of foodstuffs, makes possible the development of
industry and trade (II, 120-21). Unlike the economists of the
physiocratic school, however, Jovellanos does not consider agriculture the only source of wealth. In effect, he declares that all
wealth springs from the application of labor to a product and
that education, which improves and perfects this application, is
therefore the ultimate source of wealth (V, 7-10).

Anticipating Fisher's equation, Jovellanos sees prices as the
result of variations not only in the supply of money and the
amount of goods, but also in the velocity of the circulation of
money (II, 11). Insofar as money itself is a commodity, it has a

price like any other, so that interest, long condemned by the
Church, is neither evil nor fearsome for our author (II, 8a). We
have already seen that Jovellanos discards the medieval concept of a "just" price.

VIII   *The Significance of Jovellanos' Economic Writings*

Jovellanos' private opinions were more "advanced" than
those which he expressed in his public writings, and an examination of his doctrine must therefore be supplemented with study
of his letters and diary. Concerning the *Report on the Agrarian
Law,* he wrote a fellow member of the Economic Society of
Madrid: "I might certainly have said more about amortization,
entails, taxes, etc.; but you, who know how much must be overcome in order to accomplish anything in these matters, will perhaps think that I have rather overshot the mark. It is not enough
to see one's goal; one must not lose sight of one's starting
place" (IV, 189b-90a). In his diary, he promises to tell his
friends "why I did not propose the absolute abolition of every
kind of entail and amortization, which I consider necessary,
why I blocked free grain exports, which I consider just, and
other matters in keeping with the demands of these times" (D
II, 149). This reticence stemmed in part from Jovellanos' "writing in the name of a body which would not then have adopted
my ideas and which even now will not easily approve of them,
and whose approbation is nevertheless important, not only to
give them the weight of authority but also because only thus
can they hope for public examination and some acceptance"
(II, 367b). We have seen that even in this muted form,
Jovellanos' ideas were too radical for some of his contemporaries.

Apart from its significance in the history of Spanish economic and political thought, the *Report on the Agrarian Law* is a
masterpiece of systematic exposition, developing specific proposals from explicitly stated principles with that geometric clarity so dear to the eighteenth century. Though remarkably free
of the aridity of technical jargon, as comparison with the writings of Campomanes will show, it gives literary status to an
abundance of technical and regional terms, proving that they are

not incompatible with elegant prose.[11] As had some of his
verses, Jovellanos' *Report* foreshadows the linguistic emancipation which accompanied the Romantic revolution.

Jovellanos' economic writings were responses to specific
practical problems; and they sought solutions which, within the
realm of the feasible, would come as close as possible to the
desirable. In dealing with questions which had concerned other
Spanish writers for more than a century, Jovellanos naturally
followed, at least in part, in their footsteps; but he was not
afraid to develop new ideas and to make use of the latest economic thinking. Thus he came to advance beyond the relatively
liberal mercantilism of Campomanes and, especially after he discovered Adam Smith's *Wealth of Nations,* which he read several
times, to move ever more in the direction of classical liberalism.
Like Smith, he stressed the basic importance of agriculture in
the national economy while also recognizing the productive role
of manufactures and commerce. Jovellanos, like Smith, was
eclectic and pragmatic, applying principles to specific cases.

Jovellanos' economic thought cannot be divorced from social
and political considerations. His agrarian proposals would build
a rural middle class of independent small farmers at the expense
of the grazing interests, the nobles, and the Church. They would
produce a less rigidly stratified society and at the same time
strengthen the State by weakening the upper classes. His other
economic writings envisage a similar growth of an urban middle
class of manufacturers and merchants, freed from the restraints
and stigmas of a feudal order. Jovellanos was neither irreligious
nor egalitarian; but he thought of both Church and nobility as
functional members of society, subject to the control of the
State and not entitled to any privileges that did not contribute
to their social usefulness. The abolition of legal restraints and
the resulting growth of industry and trade would, he believed,
improve the lot of the working class, providing more jobs and a
larger share in an increased national wealth. Jovellanos' works
bear witness to his conviction that economic progress depends
on educational progress and is, in turn, only a means to social,
political, and humanitarian goals.

CHAPTER 6

Education and Philosophy

I Education and the Enlightenment

T HE heart of the Enlightenment, in Spain as in the rest of Europe, was education. The ruling classes, if they were to exercise power for their own true benefit and that of the remainder of the population, had to acquire the knowledge requisite to statesmanship: economics, history, political theory, and law. The laboring classes, if their standard of living was to rise, had to learn how to apply scientific and technical advances to agriculture and manufactures. Education seemed to be the means for the material and moral betterment of individuals and the human race. This was no matter of individual salvation and harmony with God, but a lay concept of morality envisaging the progressive and indefinite betterment of the entire species as men came increasingly to understand their true relationship to their fellowmen.[1] Such leading figures of the age as Condillac, Condorcet, Rousseau, and Locke, to name only a few, did not disdain to elaborate plans of education; and a pedagogic upheaval was initiated by Pestalozzi in the late eighteenth century. Insofar as educational innovations were put into practice, this usually occurred outside the established educational institutions. Universities in particular seem everywhere to have constituted an intellectual rear guard preserving the academic disciplines and methods of the Middle Ages. Adam Smith, for instance, considered them the last refuge of outworn and discredited systems; and he found that in the University of Oxford, most professors had long since given up all pretense of teaching (pp. 718, 727).

Like his illustrious contemporaries, Jovellanos saw in education the key to a better future. In his *Report on the Agrarian Law* he asks for the propagation of the technical knowledge requisite to economic development. In other writings and as a member of the Economic Societies, he promoted vocational training among the poor, among women, and among nuns (II, 42b-43a, 355-56). The political system which Jovellanos envisaged, permitting free expression and a free press and involving a parliament representative of the various social ranks, presupposed a progressive enlightenment of the citizenry.

Spanish education in Jovellanos' time was far from fulfilling the demands which reformers placed on it. Primary education, though widely accessible, was by no means universal, so that many peasants and laborers remained illiterate. Secondary education was limited both in its availability and its scope. It was traditionally humanistic; and the humanities, then as now, formed the individual but did not train him for an economically productive role. To prepare students for university work, which required a thorough knowledge of Latin, a large part of secondary studies was devoted to ancient languages, literatures, and history, frequently at the expense of attention to Spanish history and culture. The Jesuits had provided highly esteemed secondary schools, attended largely by the upper classes. After the expulsion of this Order in 1767, the State attempted to carry on its work while modernizing the curriculum. State schools taught such subjects as modern foreign languages, natural sciences, and what we now call "political science," a study meant to strengthen the hand of the State in its long struggle with the authority of the Church. The school established at Vergara by the Basque Economic Society, a school which Jovellanos admired and to some extent imitated in Gijón, followed a similarly modern curriculum.[2]

Universities did not enjoy the esteem of the reformers. Even the leading ones, Salamanca and Alcalá, were the butt of sarcastic remarks by Cadalso and Tomás de Iriarte (Cotarelo, pp. 127-28, 134, n. 2); and some of the less reputable ones had become little more than diploma factories. As in other countries, universities in Spain tended to resist intellectual and curricular innovation. To be sure, some important figures of the Enlightenment did have connections with them; Feijóo, for instance, was for most of his life a professor of theology at the University of Oviedo. His intellectual significance, however, has nothing to do with that position; his readings, investigations, and writings deal only tangentially with the science he professed. The important intellectual progress of the age, in Spain and elsewhere, took place outside the universities and often against their opposition. They were largely dominated by the clergy and sometimes injured by strife among the religious orders. Instruction was given in Latin. The major disciplines were the traditional ones of theology and jurisprudence and, to a lesser extent, medicine; and most of what constitutes the curriculum of today's American university was totally ignored. Diego de Torres Villarroel, in his autobiography, gives us a frightening picture of the University of Salamanca early in the century: violent factionalism split the school, and such chairs as those of mathematics, Greek, and Hebrew remained unfilled for years or even decades. The government of Charles III tried repeatedly to reform higher education, but the very repetition of such efforts is an adequate commentary on their effectiveness. As late as 1798 Jovellanos reports to Charles IV that the University of Salamanca "unfortunately still resembles an ecclesiastical establishment" (V, 294a); and in 1802 he finds "modern" studies unsuited to the universities, whose venerable institutions he wishes, with some irony, to leave undisturbed (I, 237a).

II   Jovellanos' Educational Writings

Since the Spanish educational system of the latter eighteenth century was ill-suited to carry out the tasks which Jovellanos, in common with other reformers, envisaged, he set out to change it. His efforts were both practical—the establishment of schools, notably of the Royal Asturian Institute—and theoretical—a series of pedagogical writings extending over almost three decades, from the *Discurso sobre los medios de promover la felicidad de Asturias* (*An Address on the Means of Promoting the Prosperity of Asturias*), 1781, to the *Bases para la formación de un plan general de instrucción pública* (*Bases for the Formation of a General Plan of Public Education*), 1809, and including the *Regulations for the College of Calatrava* (1790), the *Ordenanza para el Real Instituto Asturiano* (*Regulations for the Royal Asturian Institute*), 1793, various discourses written in the 1790's on the need for scientific education and the relationship between scientific and humanistic training, and the *Theoretical-Practical Treatise on Education* (1802).

In these works Jovellanos deals with the entire range of educational problems. He discusses physical and financial arrangements for the establishment and conduct of schools, practical details of housing, discipline, examinations, grading, etc., and questions of curriculum. He combines the discussion of such problems with an exposition of his opinions on epistemology and ethics, writing on philosophical questions only in connection with matters of more immediate concern.

Editions of Jovellanos' works include the *Course in Spanish Humanities*, consisting of a preliminary essay followed by sections on poetics, rhetoric, English and French grammar, and general grammar or linguistics. The desire to give humanistic training in Spanish, with the study of Spanish texts, rather than in Latin and oriented exclusively to the study of ancient literature, is characteristic of Jovellanos, as is the wish to instruct students in the grammatical rudiments of modern foreign languages. Jovellanos himself gave English lessons at the Royal Asturian Institute, as well as lectures on rhetoric and poetics; and the *Course* generally reflects the actual teaching of these subjects at the Institute under Jovellanos' direction. There are, however, reasons to question his authorship, though not his inspiration, of all but the preliminary essay, for whose authenticity we have the testimony of Jovellanos' diary.[3] I therefore choose texts clearly by Jovellanos when a subject is dealt with in more than one place.

A similar situation exists with respect to the *Plan para la educación de la nobleza* (*Plan for the Education of the Nobility*), which reflects some of Jovellanos' ideas and may be inspired by him or produced by him in collaboration with others, but which is probably not exclusively his. Its date, 1798, corresponds to the period of Jovellanos' ministry. We know that Jovellanos' official duties involved educational reform, but the *Plan* could well have been prepared by subordinates.[4]

Jovellanos' major pedagogic work, if one omits the detailed regulations for specific schools, is the *Theoretical-Practical Treatise on Education*, written in 1802, while its author was a prisoner on Majorca, for a contest sponsored by the Economic Society of that island. In this, his most extensive theoretical study of educational questions, Jovellanos argues that the prosperity of a society requires widespread free public education, the nature of which he then proceeds to outline. It is to consist of "sciences of method," that is, the tools for learning, followed by the "instructive sciences," which convey factual information. Jovellanos intended also to propose methods of financing such education, but his plan remained unfinished. The following analysis of his pedagogic and, to some extent, philosophic thought is largely based on the *Treatise* (I, 230-67).

III   *Epistemology*

Jovellanos' educational writings show him to be a resolute enemy of what his age called scholasticism; and his contemporaries recognized him as such, hoping that he would help to deliver them from "scholastic darkness" and "the chains of prejudice" (IV, 499a), or persecuting him for ideas allegedly subversive of the religious and political order.[5]

This antischolasticisim does not imply rejection of Roman Catholic theology. There is ample evidence that Jovellanos not only believed the teachings of the Church but also practiced all that the Church demands, and more. Unlike some of his detractors, however, he distinguished between religion and Church; and consequently he occasionally attacked what he considered economic and political encroachments by the Church on the public welfare and the authority of the crown. Furthermore, condemnation of scholasticism does not necessarily signify rejection of the ethical and juridical concepts of medieval Christianity, including those of St. Thomas Aquinas. Jovellanos and other moderate reformers of his time did not seek to make a clean sweep of the past, but to submit its tenets and practices to rational examination.

What Jovellanos' antischolastic posture does signify is disenchantment with the scholastic and Aristotelian *method* of teaching and learning followed by the educational establishments of his day. In practice, this method meant a tendency to interpret reality by means of deductive reasoning which started from the opinions of authorities consecrated by tradition, even when, as in the case of scientific and medical treatises, they plainly contradicted experiment and experience. It meant what Jovellanos considered an abuse of syllogistic reasoning inappropriately applied and prizing cleverness of argument above the discovery of truth (*Calatrava*, pp. 207-8). Preoccupation with method is clear in Jovellanos' condemnation of his own early training: "In my first studies I followed, without any choice, the regular method of our teachers. Afterwards I studied philosophy, always following the ordinary method and ancient topics of our schools. I began the study of jurisprudence with no preparation other than a barbarous logic and a sterile and confused metaphysics, which I thought at that time gave me a master key with which to enter the sanctuary of knowledge. Even my teachers considered all other studies, including history, to be useless" (I, 288b).

This condemnation of scholasticism extends also to theological texts. Jovellanos declares that St. Thomas' *Summa theologica*, though a great work, suffers from the uncritical scholastic methods of its author's time, besides being of little use for elementary theological studies and for the defense of the Church against its modern enemies (*Calatrava*, pp. 161-62). In all intellectual fields Aristotelian philosophy, "deformed" and "corrupted" by its Arabic and European commentators and interpreters, had become "the best shield of common prejudices" (I, 314a) and had, in effect, closed the gates of knowledge. "The glory of opening them wide was reserved for the sublime genius of Bacon" (I, 336b). Peripatetic philosophy had perverted theological studies, directing attention away from the sources (Bible, patristic writings, councils, etc.) and toward its own sophistic speculations (*Calatrava*, pp. 152-53). It had impeded the progress of natural science by confusing men with idle speculations (I, 336), which Jovellanos promises to avoid in the Asturian Institute:

In it there will be no attempt to obfuscate your minds with empty opinions or to cram them with sterile truths, no attempt to launch them on metaphysical investigations or to make them roam through those unknown regions where for so long a time they strayed. What can the presumptious rashness of man find in them? From Zeno to Spinoza and from Thales to Malebranche, what could ontology discover but monsters, chimaeras, doubts, or illusions? Ah, without revelation, without this divine light which descended from heaven to illuminate and strengthen our dark and weak reason, what would man have grasped of all that exists outside of nature? What would he have grasped even of those sacred truths which so ennoble his being and form his sweetest consolation? (I, 320a; cf. I, 314b)

The alternative to scholasticism was, for Jovellanos, the sensualistic epistemology of Locke and Condillac. "Locke restored [logic], if, indeed, he did not found it; Condillac simplified its principles; Bonnet improved them; and in my opinion our Eximeno purified and perfected them."[6] Jovellanos sees logic in Lockeian terms, not only as the play of syllogisms but as an effort to explain the origin of our ideas and the nature of the mind. Like Locke, Jovellanos believes that all ideas are derived from experience, either directly through sensation or indirectly by reflection (I, 240a); but, like Condillac, he tends to emphasize the role of sensation. "Man receives all his first ideas through the senses," he writes. "His soul perceives and compares them and operates on them."[7] Elsewhere we read: "Can we doubt that the soul thinks because it feels, and that if feeling and thinking are not one and the same thing, we must say that it feels before it thinks?"[8]

Between these views and scholasticism there is no necessary contradiction, but there are important differences in stress. The scholastics tended to revere and study authority, whereas Bacon, Locke, and Condillac drew attention toward external phenomena as perceived by the mind and toward the operations of that mind. Jovellanos admired all three of these authors, but in his own writings he seems closest to Condillac.[9] The introspective psychology which the new epistemology demanded is what Jovellanos calls logic, an extremely broad concept for him:

If its principal object [of study] are ideas, must it not investigate their nature before dealing with their relationships? And can it investigate or explain the doctrine relating to both of these matters without showing, first, what being conceives ideas; second, to what objects they refer; third, what notions may be reached by proceeding from one idea to another; fourth, and assuming that they have reached their highest point, to what new series of ideas one may descend from that point?

Someone may perhaps tell us that none of this has to do with logic, and not without some justification, in view of the common meaning of this term. But does it not have to do with the science of ideas? And is not this science the true key to all the rest, the one which ought to be set at their gate and occupy the place given to the art of reasoning? Then call it "ideology," a name which certainly suits it better; but assign to it the body of doctrine which is essentially related to its object. (I, 249a)

The term "ideology," whose invention dictionaries credit to Destutt de Tracy, was already current in French by 1776 (before the publication of the French philosopher's works), when the Spaniard Capmany defended his use of *ideología* to translate it.[10] Jovellanos, like his contemporaries, understands it to be the science of ideas. It is to deal with the nature and faculties of the soul and with the nature of sense impressions. It should also explore how the soul, though perceiving only the outer characteristics of things and never their essences and substances, can distinguish among them and understand the relations among them. Comprehension of the series of efficient and final causes that unites all things leads to knowledge and recognition of a perfect Supreme Being and, ultimately, to knowledge of the eternal moral principles "engraved in the soul" by God. "In short, our ideology must link, in the order which their very nature indicates, the main ideas of dialectics, psychology, cosmology, ontology, natural theology, and ethics; in a word, all the principles of . . . philosophy" (I, 249). Astonishingly, Jovellanos considers the study of all this a necessary preliminary to the education of young children.

IV *Ethics*

Jovellanos believes that practical moral training has been neglected. Like Condillac and Locke, he rejects the notion of innate ideas; yet he considers man to be naturally endowed with a desire and capacity for virtue from which a system of natural ethics can be derived by reason and by a moral sense. This, presumably, is the way in which moral principles are "engraved in the soul." The young must therefore be taught to develop their abilities and to recognize a hierarchy of pleasures rising from the physical through the intellectual and aesthetic to the moral. Christian ethics is for Jovellanos the perfection of natural ethics, to be inculcated through a program of religious instruction, including catechism and Bible reading.

Man has obligations to God, to himself, and to his fellowmen; and since he necessarily exists in society, his obligations to his fellowmen are inescapable. Jovellanos therefore stresses the need for training in civic morality, which, among other things, demands that each individual educate himself and his children (I, 235-36, 251 ff.). All of this ethical study is for Jovellanos a part of "ideology," that is, of the study of the self, the mind, and the operations of the mind.

V Language

Ideology, or logic, is one of the "sciences of method" which are to give students the tools for acquiring practical factual knowledge. The other such tools are language and mathematics, the latter being itself a kind of language. Like Condillac, Jovellanos considers language a method of analysis and the necessary concomitant of thought. "To think is to talk to oneself," he writes in the *Theoretical-Practical Treatise.* "Since man, in order to think, needs a collection of signs which will determine and order the different ideas of which his thoughts consist, language has become for him a true analytic tool, and the art of thought has come to coincide with the art of speech to such an extent that they have become virtually the same thing" (I, 240a; cf. II, 145b).

Clear thought therefore requires clear speech, and clear speech requires the cultivation of the language. Jovellanos wants students to be trained in their own language, in foreign languages, and in the science of language itself. This study, which Jovellanos calls general grammar and we should call linguistics, is to help the student understand the working of his own tongue. It should also prepare him for the study of foreign languages (I, 245a, 248a, 270a), which seems to me to reverse the natural order of things. Jovellanos considers Latin very useful for future lawyers and theologians; but he urges the study of modern languages, especially English and French, for those planning on "practical" careers.

And now if someone wishing to study only one of these languages should ask me which he ought to prefer, I shall tell him that French offers a body of learning which is more universal, more varied, more methodical, more agreeably expounded, and above all more closely linked with our present [1802] interests and political relations; and that English holds learning which is more original, more profound, more solid, more uniform, and, generally speaking, purer and more congenial to the Spanish character; and that, therefore, by weighing and comparing these advantages, he can choose whichever best suits his taste and his aims. I shall also say, however, that since we know both languages to be so useful for learning and other occasions in life, it will always be best for anyone aspiring to perfect his education to make an effort to study both. (I, 248a)

Jovellanos' special attention is devoted to the native language. Students should receive thorough training in Spanish grammar; and their work in rhetoric and poetics, intended to increase the effectiveness of their use of language as well as to open areas of aesthetic pleasure, ought to be done, unlike traditional humanistic training, entirely in Spanish. Spanish writers, or, if necessary, Spanish translations of Classical writers, should furnish the models for study and imitation; and such study should stress careful reading and comprehension of texts, not their memorization (I, 244 ff.). Spanish, furthermore, should be the sole language of instruction, not only on the secondary level but also in the universities, whose continued use of Latin Jovellanos calls irrational and impractical (I, 237a, 270-71; II, 145a).

What we call "Spanish" is of course not the native language of all Spaniards; and Jovellanos, himself the son of a dialectal region, favored cultivating the forms of local speech and giving them the dignity and precision of the literary language. Thus in the *Theoretical-Practical Treatise*, written in Majorca for the Majorcan Economic Society, he recommends training in the Majorcan language, a variety of Catalan (I, 245b); and in Gijón he worked for the establishment of a local academy and the preparation of a dictionary of *bable*, the archaic Asturian dialect. In his appreciation of local linguistic tradition Jovellanos foreshadows the Romantic penchant for the national, the local, the specific and separate. From a different perspective, he may be seen as trying to perform for the minor languages of Spain the same service which three hundred years earlier Antonio de Nebrija had performed for Castilian, or "Spanish": to give them cultural parity with the learned and official languages.

VI   *Mathematics and the Natural Sciences*

Jovellanos values mathematics as an "algebraic language" in which signs correspond exactly to ideas. Only by imitating this precision can the other intellectual sciences be "elevated" into the class of "demonstrative sciences" (I, 250b). The *Theoretical-Practical Treatise* breaks off before discussing mathematical studies in detail, but Jovellanos' other writings give evidence of his predilection for algebraic and geometric studies. He considers geometry "the true logic of man, since by occupying him in the demonstration of definite undoubted truths and accustoming him to the rejection of any idea that is not precise, clear, and distinct, it is the one [logic] which truly teaches him to think with order and precision and to reject the errors which he finds on his way" (II, 146a). This admiration for the "geometric spirit" and for mathematics as a model of human knowledge is characteristic of the Enlightenment.

Mastery of the "sciences of method" was to be followed, according to the *Theoretical-Practical Treatise*, by study of the "instructive sciences," in which, to judge by Jovellanos' other works, a large role must have been allotted to those subjects which would contribute to economic development: pure and applied natural sciences, economics, and business management.

VII   Bases for a Plan of Education *and* Regulations for the College of Calatrava

Jovellanos' other pedagogical writings present much the same ideas as the *Treatise*, modified as times and circumstances dictated. Thus the *Bases for the Formation of a General Plan of Public Education*, prepared in 1809 during the struggle against Bonaparte, stresses the duty of the schools to inculcate "love of country, hatred of tyranny, subordination to lawful authority, beneficence, a desire for peace and public order, and all the social virtues which form good and generous citizens and which raise public morality, without which no state can be secure or free and prosperous" (I, 272a). Likewise, although he had earlier considered physical training to be the province of parents, Jovellanos now urges that it be made compulsory for all students in the public establishments and combined with basic military training (I, 268-69).

In a class by themselves are the *Regulations for the College of Calatrava*, a training institution for priests. Theological and canonical studies are naturally stressed in Jovellanos' plan for this college. Humanities are important as part of general training in language and as preparation in the Latin required for the specialized work of the college. The scientific and technical subjects which Jovellanos favored in lay institutions are correspondingly omitted.

In the *Regulations*, as in his other writings, Jovellanos expresses his aversion to scholastic methods and his preference for the epistemology of Locke and Condillac. Here also he shows his distrust of the Spanish universities; although the college was a private adjunct to the University of Salamanca, Jovellanos declares the course of studies in the public university to be almost useless and often worse than useless, since it diverts the students' attention from more sensibly organized and therefore more profitable work (p. 155). The college's students obtained their degrees from the university, but clearly they were to receive most of their significant instruction within the college and according to methods and textbooks sharply divergent from those of the university. Jovellanos' advocacy of some modern texts led to accusations, since shown to be ill-founded, that he was propagating heretical doctrines.[11]

The College of Calatrava, like other institutions with which Jovellanos concerned himself, was to use Spanish rather than Latin as the language of instruction. Careful reading and comprehension of texts was to replace memorization. Students were to be treated humanely; physical brutality was proscribed, as always in Jovellanos' pedagogical writings; and the psychological brutality of senseless humiliations was to be replaced with an intelligent system of rewards and punishments designed to encourage each student to work at his best level of achievement.

VIII   *The Royal Asturian Institute*

Jovellanos' greatest practical accomplishment in the realm of education was the Royal Asturian Institute of Navigation and

Mineralogy. Like many of Jovellanos' writings, this school was a
direct response to specific problems. The population of Asturias
pressed heavily on the available agricultural land. Alternative
sources of employment and prosperity were at hand in the fish-
eries and seagoing commerce as well as in the coal industry, at
that time still in its infancy. Both navigation and mining, however, required development of the province's technical resources.
As early as 1781, in his *Address on the Means of Promoting the
Prosperity of Asturias,* Jovellanos had urged intensive study of
mathematics, economics, and physical sciences; and the next
year he proposed sending two young men to study in Vergara
and abroad in order afterwards to teach science and mathematics in a school for the Asturian nobility (I, 303b-4a; II, 451-
52). At Vergara the Basque Economic Society had established a
seminary in which young men of good family received the modern instruction favored by its enlightened founders. Although it
came to be suspected of harboring heretical and subversive ideas,
Vergara served as a model for Jovellanos' evolving concept of
an Asturian Institute.

After his banishment in 1790, Jovellanos tried unsuccessfully
to return to Madrid as director of the Reales Estudios de San
Isidro, a government-operated secondary institution.[12] In Gijón,
meanwhile, he devoted himself ever more assiduously to the creation of a technical school. He had the support of the Navy Minister, Antonio Valdés, and of his brother, Francisco de Paula de
Jovellanos, one of the town's leading citizens, who donated a
house near the fine old stone mansion of the Jovellanos family.
This original home of the Institute still stands on the Plaza
de Jovellanos, in Gijón; and there the school was inaugurated
on January 7, 1794, with an oration by Don Gaspar (I, 318-24),
concerning which he comments in his diary: "The speech began
at nine. I was quite calm; and to judge by the effects, it was well
read, because it drew some tears of tenderness. I myself often
felt forced to hold them back; and now and then I had to interrupt it, though with a great increase of general interest" (D I,
370).

The school which opened with such a typically eighteenth-
century effusion of tears on the occasion of promoting utility
was what we should call a technical high school. The students

ranged in age from thirteen to over twenty, with some auditors as young as ten (II, 397-98). Their studies, directed toward practical application in mining and navigation, were broader than the purely professional ones of the specialized military schools; but they were technical, i. e., applied, rather than "scientific" for their own sake.[13] Like Locke, Jovellanos believed that human knowledge has limits which it is folly to attempt to transgress (I, 322b, 340b; II, 413a, 415a). The motto he chose for the Institute, *Quid verum, quid utile*, reflects the dual goal he set for the school: to seek useful truth, and true usefulness. Jovellanos did not preach the pursuit of truth for its own sake.

The curriculum of the Royal Asturian Institute, as codified in its *Ordenanza* (*Ordinances*, II, 399-420; cf. I, 617b-18a; II, 389b), was weighted in favor of mathematics and the physical sciences; but it did not exclude other subjects that contributed to the formation of the man and the technician. The boys therefore studied humanities, including grammar, rhetoric, and poetics; but this instruction was given entirely in Spanish and with Spanish examples and models. English and French were also taught, largely to facilitate the translation of modern technical publications. Jovellanos himself, while in Gijón, helped in the teaching of these languages. In addition, the students learned technical drawing.

Jovellanos meant the Institute to serve as a model for other technical institutions (I, 325b; II, 202a, 266b). It was also a step in the further laicization of Spanish education. It taught no Latin, prepared students for no university courses, such as canon law or theology, and was financed and operated by laymen with the support of the government. The Institute pioneered in generally modern and humane methods of instruction and discipline. Rote learning was to be held to a minimum; the school would stimulate and utilize the students' desire to learn; corporal punishments were prohibited; the importance of recreation was recognized. Even so, Jovellanos' program for the Institute may seem antiquated in part and demanding far beyond the level of most of our schools; but it comes as a pleasant surprise to anyone familiar with descriptions of the traditional Spanish institutions, even if we discount half of what we are told by such authors as Torres Villarroel and Quevedo. Jovellanos' approach

to education seems to have made a favorable impression on
Manuel Godoy, who made him Minister of Justice partly to
promote educational reform and who, in 1806, even with
Jovellanos imprisoned in Bellver, established a Pestalozzian institute in Madrid.[14]

The Royal Asturian Institute was immediately recognized as
an innovation in Spanish education. It was generously supported
by enlightened elements, including members of the clergy; but
it also attracted the unfavorable attention of the Inquisition and
the hostility of those, clergy and laity, who saw anything "modern" as subversive of Altar and Throne. A new and larger building was constructed for it beginning in 1797, according to the
plans of the architect Juan de Villanueva. This building continued to be the home of the Institute, since renamed Royal
Jovellanos Institute, until the 1960's. After Jovellanos' imprisonment in 1801 the Institute fell upon hard times; its vicissitudes
need not concern us here, except to note that after its pioneering years it became indistinguishable from other Spanish *ins-
titutos.*

Jovellanos also tried to improve the primary education of
Gijón. He was instrumental in the establishment of a free
elementary school for poor boys, with funds willed for this purpose by a friend, Don Fernando Morán-La Bandera; and he
persuaded one of his sisters to found a similar school for
girls (Ceán, pp. 227-29; Somoza, *Documentos,* I, 173).

IX   *The Significance of Jovellanos' Work in Education*

Both in theory and in practice Jovellanos concerned himself
with education during all his mature life. Indeed, one of his last
writings is an appeal for funds to restore the Institute, which
had suffered from official neglect and French vandalism (V,
261-62). In theory and in practice he was a champion of a modern utilitarian education, designed to raise the economic level of
his countrymen; but he also insisted on the necessity of forming
the taste and spirit by means of humanistic studies. This man of
the Enlightenment, a period so long and so foolishly condemned
as "Frenchified," stressed the importance of the native language,
the national literature, and national history and juridical traditions.

In epistemology Jovellanos' writings reflect the sensualism of the modern British and French thinkers. His concepts of moral sense and the cult of virtue derive in part from the school of Shaftesbury, Smith, and, most directly, Hutcheson. His epistemology is applied to educational theory; his ethics is a vital part of the formation of the citizen.

In fact, all of Jovellanos' educational writing rests on a conception of the individual as a part of society, so that the progress of society requires the education of the individual and the welfare of the individual requires that he be taught to live in society. Unlike the foreign pedagogical theorists, such as Locke and Rousseau, whom he occasionally draws on, Jovellanos is interested in making education broadly available in order to raise the level of society as a whole; his pedagogical works always concern themselves with schools, not with the private tutoring of a single privileged boy. They, and the Institute he founded, had some influence in the educational reforms of the nineteenth century, though perhaps less than has sometimes been claimed. Jovellanos had not been long in the grave before it became fashionable to invoke his name without troubling to read or understand his works. What interests us today in his pedagogical writings is their role as keystone of the arch of Jovellanos' political, economic, and social thought. The Spain he wished for could only be achieved through education; and as he concerned himself with education, Jovellanos never lost sight of education's social purpose.

CHAPTER 7

Politics

I *Jovellanos' Political Writings*

JOVELLANOS had been trained in the law and he tended to view what we call "political science" as at best a pseudo-science, since it rested heavily on speculation instead of positive texts and facts (I, 102a). Nevertheless the great work of reform which busied Enlightenment Spain forced its champions to face problems of political theory and political organization. Attempted economic reforms, efforts to reshape the country's educational system, and the protracted struggle between Church and State raised questions concerning the rights of individuals and institutions; and the resolution of the conflicting claims forced the reformers to review their concept of society and their notions of the nature, functions, rights, and duties of society's components. Little wonder, then, that during the same period the study of natural law was made compulsory in the Spanish higher schools and universities by government action.

Several of Jovellanos' works, particularly those concerned with economics, deal tangentially with political theory. The best example is the *Report on the Agrarian Law*, which involves the privileges and consequently the status of the clergy and the nobility. Jovellanos, however, came to concern himself directly with political questions as a result of the War of Independence. Returning to the continent from his imprisonment on Majorca, he found Spain embarked on the struggle against Bonaparte. After some vacillation, and at the insistence of his Asturian compatriots, he became a member of the Junta Suprema Central Gubernativa de España e Indias (the Supreme Central Governing Commission of Spain and America), the provisional government created by the local committees that had sprung up all over the country. With French troops already occupying large parts of

Spain, the Junta Central seemed to have its hands full with the military problem of resisting the conqueror of all Europe. It was, however, also forced to deal with fundamental political issues. For one thing, there were those who challenged its legitimacy and sought to limit, if not undermine, its authority. For another, the turmoil of the moment, the collapse of the established government, and the improvisation of local and national alternatives all raised, explicitly or implicitly, the question of what kind of political system should follow peace.

Jovellanos dealt with these issues as a member of the Junta Central; and he played a leading part in the debates that preceded the convening of the *cortes* (parliament) of 1810, a body which, while professing its esteem for him, moved from the beginning in a direction more radical than anything advocated by Don Gaspar. The Junta Central gave way to a regency on February 1, 1810; but although Jovellanos thereupon had no direct role in government, he continued to follow the debates with interest and to comment on them. Throughout these years of the War of Independence Jovellanos maintained a correspondence with a young English Whig, Lord Holland, who provided him with information about the workings of the British system of government and possibly with some guidance in the framing of proposals for reform in Spain. This correspondence (IV, 345-479) gives us valuable insight into Jovellanos' political positions under the pressure of military and political events.

Upon the dissolution of the Junta Central Jovellanos and his colleagues became the targets of the most serious charges. Stimulated by his sense of obligation to the public as well as his outraged sense of honor and dignity, Jovellanos wrote his *Memoria en defensa de la Junta Central* (*Defense of the Junta Central*), I, 503-622, published in 1811. Like most of Jovellanos' writings, it is a response to specific circumstances and particular problems; and it is Jovellanos' most extensive work on political theory and practice. Part I defends the Junta and its members against the accusations of usurpation of authority, misappropriation of public funds, and (incredible as the accusation may seem to us) treason. Part II is a personal vindication, recounting Jovellanos' liberation from prison, his rejection of the offers made to him by the Bonapartists, his participation in the work of the Junta Central, and his conduct and persecutions since the dissolution of that body. Twenty-six appendices reproduce documents related to all of these matters. They include reports written by Jovellanos on constitutional questions, either in his own name or in that of committees of which he was a member. Any attempt to characterize Jovellanos' political thought must rely heavily on this work, supplementing it with other writings, especially the economic and pedagogical.

II   *The Origin of Society*

One of the great issues in the political debates of the seventeenth and eighteenth centuries is the origin of society. Have men always lived in society, or did they at some point create society to take the place of a previous "state of nature"? The answer to this question affected the concepts of the nature of society and of men's rights and obligations within it. This relationship is perhaps best visible in John Locke's *Two Treatises of Government*, in which extensive discussion of the origin and nature of society is eventually linked to the problems raised by the English Revolution of 1688. Locke postulated a presocial state of nature, as did Hobbes, Hutcheson, and Rousseau. These writers believe in the anarchic state of man before the formation of societies, though they hold different concepts and valuations of this state; and they all ascribe the formation of society to a contract or compact, explicit or implicit. Another school of thought is represented by Adam Ferguson, whom Jovellanos greatly esteemed[1] and who declares the "state of nature" to be a fiction not only unsupported by any historical record but actually contrary to nature. Man, according to Ferguson, lives naturally in society, without any compact or contract.[2] There are variations on these themes; but the above are, in outline, the main schools of thought. Most Spaniards held the Lockeian view, rejecting both Hobbes's concept of a natural state of anarchic violence and Rousseau's condemnation of civilization.[3]

In the *Theoretical-Practical Treatise on Education*, Jovellanos declares that "society [is] the natural state of man, . . . because whatever poets and pseudophilosophers may say, history and experience never show him to us except joined in some association, be it more or less imperfect" (I, 253a). Nevertheless, he occasionally speaks of the formation of society as though it were an historical occurrence, because, believing that the needs of men are the causes of society's existence, he slips into expressions which give these causes a temporal priority over their effect.

Jovellanos, perhaps because his legal training led him to respect the importance of positive law, rejects the thesis that the political rights of man in society, his only natural state, can be based on rights which he might have possessed in a presocial condition (I, 255). He also rejects the notion that the "noble savage" is morally superior to civilized man and that the road to human betterment leads through the abolition of societies. Probably alluding to Rousseau, and writing after the French Revolution had convinced enlightened men of the dangers of certain lines of thought, he condemns such ideas as

the abortive offspring of the pride of a few impious men who, abhorring all submission to authority, sought their glory and their advantage in the subversion of every social order, under the specious guise of cosmopolitanism; and by tinting their antisocial and antireligious ideas with humanitarianism they seek to deceive the unwary, whose consolation they give the appearance of desiring and whose wretchedness and destruction they secretly plan. Enemies that they are of all religion and all authority, conspiring to encompass in the destruction of thrones and altars all institutions and all social virtues, there is no generous and beneficent idea, no virtuous and pure sentiment, but they have declared war upon it and sought to wipe it from the spirits of men. Humanity sounds forever on their lips, and the hatred and desolation of the human race secretly rages within their hearts. (I, 254b-55a)

We shall see that Jovellanos believes the relations between governors and governed to be regulated by a compact, tacit or explicit; but this compact or constitution does not create society.

III   *The Nature of Society*

Whatever may have been the origin of society, it functions, Jovellanos believes, by means of the sacrifices of its individual constituent parts. The partial sacrifice of individual freedom creates the public authority; the sacrifice of the strength of the citizen gives birth to the power of the State; and the sacrifice of individual wealth yields the public revenues. The State, in turn,

is obliged to guarantee the individual the full enjoyment of all
the remainder of those possessions (I, 256a). Thus in Jovellanos'
concept the individual has certain residual rights, and government is justified in its demands on the citizen only by its purpose, which is to safeguard all that its demands leave the individual. We are reminded of the Lockeian and Jeffersonian view of a
government existing to protect life, liberty, and property (or
"the pursuit of happiness").

The social structure is held together, according to Jovellanos,
by *el amor público*, "public spirit" or love of the common good
(I, 256b). The foundation of political power is consequently
moral, and Jovellanos declares that "the power and force of a
State consists not so much in the multitude and wealth of its
inhabitants as in their moral character" (I, 492b). Jovellanos'
formulation of this idea, in itself far from novel, seems to derive
from Adam Ferguson (*History of Civil Society,* p. 92). Furthermore, by moral character both Ferguson and Jovellanos mean
virtue, not military virtues, as did Bacon.[4] For Jovellanos, the
purpose of society ought also to be moral. It should not merely
punish vice, but promote a positive concept of virtue (V, 414).

Fundamental to these ideas is a view of society as an organ-
ism whose parts coexist harmoniously in a careful balance of
functions. Each part is equally a member of the whole, yet no
two parts are quite alike in their capacities and obligations.
Jovellanos believes in the brotherhood of all men and in their
equality before God, before nature, and before and within the
law. Alongside this basic equality, however, Jovellanos accepts
and justifies functional inequality. Society, he believes, necessarily means hierarchy, not because of differences in ultimate
value, but because their capacities and position oblige some men
to lead and others to follow (I, 256a). This view, akin to that
put forth in our own century by José Ortega y Gasset, is best
exemplified in Jovellanos' comments on the nobility.

The eighteenth century increasingly questioned the social justification of the privileges of a class which had been replaced in
warfare by professional soldiers and in administration by middle-
class bureaucrats. In Spain, the various noble ranks constituted
almost a twentieth of the population, more than twice the proportion which existed in pre-Revolutionary France (Herr, p. 95,
n. 13). They were exempt from most taxes, though they pos-

sessed well over five percent of the nation's wealth. They devoted many acres of land to game preserves, parks, and similar unproductive uses; and even the poorer ones among them were discouraged from work by the rules of their caste. As a class, therefore, the nobility contributed less than its just share to the economic development of Spanish society, yet some of its members felt entitled to the support of that society and proposed the establishment of a *montepío* or welfare fund for destitute nobles in Madrid. Jovellanos' report on this proposal (II, 14-19, 1784), though short, reveals his attitudes toward this class.

Jovellanos himself was proud of belonging to a noble family, but he considered nobility an artificial and arbitrary creation of society (II, 14a, 106b). Medieval society had established it for the specific purpose of defense and, through its privileges, assured it the wealth that would allow it to devote itself entirely to its function (II, 14b, 16). The noble is not biologically superior to the commoner, though environment may produce a moral superiority that Jovellanos explains in the *Report on the Agrarian Law*:

It is an undeniable truth that virtue and talents are not linked to birth or class, and that for this reason it would be a grave injustice to bar some classes from service and its rewards. Nevertheless, it is as difficult to expect valor, integrity, elevation of spirit and all the other great qualities which great positions demand, from an obscure and poor upbringing or from employments whose constant exercise shrinks the spirit, presenting it with no stimulus but necessity, no goal but self-interest, as it is easy to find those qualities in the midst of the abundance, the splendor, and even the prejudices of those families which are accustomed to prefer honor to comfort and to seek their fortunes only in glory and reputation. (II, 105b)

Nevertheless, the noble, as Jovellanos paints him in the 1790's and as he had already depicted him in his Second Satire, is an example more of vices than of virtues:

The most common [vice] is that of those nobles who, believing that their nobility relieves them of all obligations, apply themselves to nothing, learn nothing, and in no way make themselves useful to society; who believe that all were born to serve and adore them, that the laws were not made for them, that the ministers of religion and of justice have no right to punish or reprehend them, that their houses ought to be the asylum of all who seek their protection, that luxury and idleness ought to live with them, that frugality and work are virtues of the mob; who are proud, oppressive, discourteous, deceitful, etc.; and [who believe], in short, that the splendor of their family and their name authorizes them to be proud, insolent, oppressive, deceitful, and disorderly. (IV, 185)

This moral decay of the nobility destroys mutual respect and affection among the social classes. Jovellanos' diary gives us an insight into this social dissolution when it describes popular reaction to an accident:

The whole town came to help the coachmen and did so with remarkable diligence and charity; but—a notable thing!—not a single man cared about us or helped us with his compassion or even asked us whether we had been hurt. Is this not proof of the prejudice with which all who have the air of gentlemen about them are viewed? Man, yearning always to recover his natural equality, looks with pleasure on the sufferings of those who disturb it and with the same pleasure helps those who are on his level, since he considers them alone as his fellow creatures. (D I, 226)

The diary also shows how odious and unfounded differentiation among men can spread through all social levels. It describes an Asturian community in which the nobles have preferred seats in church, with the acquiescence of the commoners, who in turn exclude from church altogether a nomadic caste called *vaqueros de alzada.* These unfortunates must receive communion at the church door. Appalled by this system, Jovellanos asks: "When will Heaven avenge the greater part of the human race for such scandalous and ridiculous distinctions? I am ashamed," he adds, "to live in a country that has nurtured them and that promotes them; but in the end, reason will some day take revenge for the insults that today it receives from ignorance" (D I, 309-10).

In his report on the proposed welfare fund for nobles, Jovellanos argues that a rich noble may or may not be useful to society; but a poor noble, who cannot create for his descendants the environment which breeds greatness, and who is incompetent or unwilling to perform any useful service, has no claim to be supported by society. If, in order to eat, he must accept employment which costs him his rank, society loses an idle member and gains a productive one. Jovellanos therefore rejects the proposed *montepío.*

Those nobles, however, who have the means of subsistence ought also to reflect on their position in society and to do something to justify it. At the height of the French Revolution

Jovellanos inaugurates the Royal Asturian Institute and calls the nobles to it:

The people that supports you needs your guidance and your knowledge. If its helplessness should not move you to come to its aid, let at least your own interest and the decorum of your class move you. You are no longer, as you were in other times, the only bulwarks of the nation's security, nor the defenders of its rights, nor the interpreters of its will. Your escutcheons and your privileges are no longer based on such sound claims; only true patriotism, only virtue, an enlightened and beneficent virtue, can justify and preserve them. Come, teach the people, help it, and pay with your knowledge and advice for that sweat which it constantly sheds on your lands, that innocent and precious sweat to which you owe your splendor and your very existence. (I, 323a)

Here Jovellanos calls on his class, displaced from warfare and government, to reassert its leadership in society in the modern terms of education and economic progress and development.

IV *The Spanish Constitution*

These ideas on the origin and nature of society, on the function of government, and on the relations among the social classes were all brought to bear on the constitutional questions which especially concerned Jovellanos in his last years. Such questions were much debated in the Spain of the latter eighteenth century. Most Enlightened thinkers believed in the existence of a medieval Spanish constitution, destroyed by the absolutism of subsequent monarchs (Herr, pp. 341-47). They disagreed on its nature, the precise causes of its decline, and the desirability and means of restoring it. Such debates paralleled similar discussions in foreign countries, which produced such outstanding works as the *Two Treatises of Government* of John Locke and the *Esprit des lois* of Montesquieu. Both of these writers had their influence in Spain, and Jovellanos knew the works of both. This period also produced various constitutions devised by the revolutionaries in France, as well as the oldest written constitution still in effect, our own.

Both America and France tended to identify a constitution with a written document produced at a specific time. Thomas Paine, for instance, declared that a constitution "has not an ideal, but a real existence; and wherever it cannot be produced in a visible form, there is none."[5] One can, however, like Edmund

Burke, also think of a constitution as a body of custom growing slowly in the context of history.[6] This is the view held by Adam Ferguson, who declares that "no constitution is formed by consent, no government is copied from a plan" (*History of Civil Society*, p. 188), and who stresses the historical and evolutionary nature of government and governmental institutions.

Jovellanos' interest in these questions extended over many years. In the 1780's his "Reflexiones sobre la constitución, las leyes, usos y costumbres de Castilla" ("Reflections on the Constitution, Laws, Usages, and Customs of Castile") protest against the excessive importance given to Roman law in Spanish legal studies and explain that humanistic and scientific training, and especially historical learning, are the keys to understanding the development of the Spanish legal system.[7] In a letter dated 1795, Jovellanos stresses the urgency of studying the Spanish constitution, that is, the distribution of governmental powers and the rights and duties of both governors and governed (II, 147).

With the French invasion of 1808 these questions became urgent. At least two distinct elements were involved in the resistance to Bonaparte. One, which included such leading figures of the Spanish Enlightenment as the Count of Floridablanca, minister under Charles III and Charles IV, sought to defend the old regime of Enlightened Despotism against military aggression and revolutionary innovations. The other faction consisted of the heirs of the Enlightenment. They were influenced by the revolutionary currents of the previous twenty or thirty years, and some of them were not greatly opposed to Bonaparte on doctrinal grounds; but they fought him in the name of national independence. They opened the liberal-Romantic-nationalistic nineteenth century, while their generally older opponents belonged to the golden age of Spanish Enlightenment, the reign of Charles III. The War of Independence was thus a two-fold struggle; even as the nation fought to liberate its territory, it reshaped its political institutions.

Jovellanos approached the constitutional problems of the War of Independence with a firm belief in the existence of a Spanish constitution, rooted, like all the others of Europe, in custom (I, 598b-99a). With this historically oriented, "organic" concept went a preference for gradual, evolutionary change, perhaps best expressed in a letter to Lord Holland:

[There is] no one more inclined [than I] to restore and strengthen and improve, no one more timid in changes and innovations. Perhaps this is already a failing of my old age. I am very suspicious of political theories, and even more of abstract ones. I believe that each nation has its character, the result of its ancient institutions; that if this character declines because of them it is also restored by them; that new times do not necessarily demand new institutions, but a modification of the old; that the important thing is to perfect education and improve our public schooling. With it every prejudice will fall, every error will disappear, every improvement will be facilitated. In conclusion: a nation needs nothing but the right to assemble and to speak. If it is educated, its liberty can always gain [from this right], never lose. (IV, 377)

Jovellanos believed that the purpose of the Junta Central and of the parliament whose convocation it prepared was not to create a new constitution but to adapt the old one to new circumstances (I, 548b-49a).

The outlines of such adaptive reform are given by Jovellanos in his *Defense of the Junta Central* (I, 549-50). There he envisages a government of separate and balanced powers. The full executive power, including the veto over legislation, belongs to the king. The legislative power is shared by the two chambers of a national parliament, with an elected lower house initiating laws and an upper house, representing the clergy and nobility, approving them. Jovellanos saw the bicameralism of the British and American legislatures as a felicitous combination of popular representation and conservative restraint. Unknown to the ancients and rejected by "the modern political theorists whose democratic propensity has caused so many evils in our age," it is the basis of Anglo-Saxon greatness and liberty and "the most precious discovery that we owe to the study of and meditation upon the ancient and modern history of societies." An independent judiciary completes Jovellanos' vision of government, though he does not conceive of it as being empowered to interpret laws (I, 512a).

Though Jovellanos purported merely to be restating some principles and features of the ancient Spanish constitution, his ideas are in several respects innovations derived from British practice. Spain had never had a national parliament; the old

cortes had been *cortes* of Castile or of Aragon, not of Spain.
The bicameral system was also alien to Spanish tradition.
Furthermore, the old *cortes*, like other parliaments, had granted
money to the crown; but they did not initiate legislation.[8]
Jovellanos' admiration for the British constitution (see I, 573b,
n. 26) led him into positions which, while too liberal for the adherents of the old regime, proved not liberal enough for the
younger element.

When the first national parliament convened in Cadiz in
1810, it organized itself in a single chamber and declared itself
the repository of sovereignty; and the Constitution of 1812,
product of those *cortes* and manifesto of Spanish liberalism,
proclaimed that sovereignty resides in the nation. Already in
1809, Jovellanos had denounced the concept of national sovereignty, declaring that in every monarchical state sovereignty
resides necessarily in the king (I, 597b). The problem was in part
terminological: Jovellanos identified sovereignty with the power
to execute the laws, while the *cortes* saw it as the power to
make the laws (Camacho, pp. 178-79).

In the next two years, Jovellanos moved to reconcile and explain these two positions. In a letter to Lord Holland he declares
that the concept of national sovereignty destroys the Spanish
constitution; but he adds that in theory it is generally accepted,
even though currently inopportune for practical reasons (IV,
473a). And in a long note to the *Defense of the Junta Central*
(I, 619-21), Jovellanos writes that even though each society
originally holds a supreme power, "the name sovereignty does
not properly fit this absolute power, because the word sovereignty is relative, and just as it implies authority and command on
one side, it implies submission and obedience on the other, so
that it can never be said with rigorous accuracy that a man or a
people is sovereign over itself." A people subject to a hereditary
monarchy, even if it has reserved to itself the legislative authority, can in no sense be called "sovereign," because sovereignty
is an attribute of the executive and is indivisible.

At this point, however, Jovellanos shifts his ground to accom-
modate the new theory, declaring it inconceivable that a society
would bestow the executive power on one person or a few, permanently and without limits or conditions.

Once these limits are prescribed, then, and these conditions are set in a constitution established by express compact or accepted by free acknowledgment, if we assume in the depositaries of this authority a perpetual right to exercise it within the bounds of the constitution, we must also assume in them a perpetual obligation not to transgress those bounds; and since the rights and obligations of contracts are relative and reciprocal, so that one cannot conceive of a right for one party that does not imply an obligation for the other, nor an obligation which does not imply a reciprocal right, the result is that if the nation thus constituted has a perpetual obligation to acknowledge and obey that power as long as it acts according to the conditions of the compact, it will also have a perpetual right to contain it within those bounds and, consequently, thus to oblige it if in fact it should transgress them; and if [the] obstinacy [of the government] were such that it should dare to maintain such a breach with force, the nation will also have the right to resist it with force and, as a last resort, to abrogate in turn a compact already openly violated by the other party, thus regaining its original rights.

According to Jovellanos, this natural right has been traditionally claimed and exercised by the Spanish nation. In order to avoid conflicting terminology, Jovellanos proposes to call it "national supremacy." In the course of his discussion, he employs arguments, which elsewhere he would have rejected, based on natural rights independent of society and positive law. In this he may reflect Locke's arguments for a "Supream Power" residing in the people and entitling them to "remove or alter the Legislative, when they find the Legislative act contrary to the trust reposed in them."[9]

V Revolution

Jovellanos was no revolutionary. His correspondence with the English radical Alexander Jardine, reflected in diary entries and a fragmentary draft, repeatedly calls for gradual progress within the limits of the possible and expresses horror at the violence of the French Revolution.[10] In the *Theoretical-Practical Treatise on Education*, Jovellanos claims that all governments can be improved and that therefore all revolutions against legitimate authority are wrong (I, 255b). When he landed on the continent in 1808 after his imprisonment on Majorca he was clearly frightened by the popular uprisings against Bonaparte (IV, 158a). Yet out of these uprisings grew the local *juntas* and, eventually, the

Junta Central, while Charles IV and Ferdinand VII had abdicated in favor of Bonaparte, whose rights were supported by a number of *Spanish* authorities. Jovellanos, swept up in the patriotic wave and carried into power, only to be accused with his colleagues of having usurped that power, was forced to justify the existence of the Junta Central. In doing so, he continues to deny that a people has any ordinary right of insurrection; but he conceives of circumstances that would justify revolution and finds precedents in medieval legislation. According to this view, a people under foreign attack and abandoned by its rulers, or a people whose legitimate government is destroyed and replaced by a tyrannical one, has the right to revolt and to determine its own fate (I, 509b, 584b). The case is that of the Spanish people in 1808; but the arguments are those with which Locke, in his *Two Treatises of Government*, justifies the English revolution of 1688, the result, according to the partisans of William and Mary, of an analogous situation (pp. 424 ff.).

VI   *Democracy*

Not only was Jovellanos generally out of sympathy with revolution; he was not a democrat, if "democracy" still has any meaning in an age of participatory democracy, people's democracy, guided democracy, organic democracy, and similar offenses against reason and language. On at least two occasions Jovellanos refers to the "democratic mania" (II, 377a; IV, 477b); and in 1809 he writes of the danger of drifting toward democracy, "a thing which not only every good Spaniard, but every right-thinking man must view with horror in a large, rich, and industrious nation of twenty-five million men scattered over such vast and separated hemispheres" (I, 596b). Yet these statements must be understood in the context of their time. "Democracy," for Jovellanos and his contemporaries, meant the direct control of "the people" over public affairs. This is how Montesquieu understood it when he elaborated his theory of the suitability of different governmental systems for nations of different sizes. According to this theory, democracy, in which all men share power, can function only within a small territory, like the Swiss republics; and the larger the state, the more concentrated power must be. The men of the Enlightenment feared that democracy would decline into mob rule, a fear which events in France did not allay. Furthermore, they were not inclined to yield power to a people which their program of reform assumed to be ignorant and incompetent (Sánchez Agesta, *Pensamiento politico,* p. 210).

Jovellanos credited the people (meaning the masses) with fundamentally good instincts, but considered it prone to be led always by others (I, 569a). Yet he was always concerned for its welfare and, indeed, its freedom, though not necessarily in a political sense (I, 312b). In his *Report on the Agrarian Law* and in that on the *Regulation of Spectacles and Public Entertainments* he calls for fewer restrictions on the innocent diversions of the masses (I, 491-93; II, 134b); and even while explaining the conformity of medieval legislation with the constitution of that time, he criticizes what he considers the chief defect of that constitution: "But above all, I seek a free people in this constitution and do not find it. Between its weakened princes and the independent feudal lords, what was the people but a flock of slaves destined to satisfy the ambition of its masters?" (I, 295).

Before his imprisonment, Jovellanos, as a government official, defended the supremacy of the civil authority over that of the Church, and that of the central government over local authorities and even local legal systems (V, 194a, 245b; D II, 458-59). He shared the presuppositions of Enlightened Despotism: that reform was necessary but could be properly guided only from above, and that division of authority was a hindrance to progress. In the *Defense of the Junta Central*, however, the government is assumed to be responsible to the people. The work itself is an accounting, and Jovellanos expects that the members of the Junta will have to give a further account to the nation assembled in parliament. The events of 1808 had shattered the old system and shown the vigor and necessity of local popularly-based organisms.

Under the first impression of those events Jovellanos wrote one of his noblest letters. Cabarrús, the friend for whom he had, in 1790, willingly incurred official wrath, had sided with the new king Joseph Bonaparte and now urged Jovellanos to collaborate in the building of a new and better Spain. Don Gaspar indignantly rejects the charge that Spain is fighting only for the Bourbons; she fights, he declares, for her rights, her constitution, her laws, and her liberty. She has recognized Ferdinand as her king; "but if force detains him or deprives her of her prince, will she not know how to seek another governor? And if she should fear that the ambition or the weakness of a king may expose her to evils as great as those she now suffers, will she not know how to live without a king and how to govern herself?" (IV, 343b). This passage has been subjected to various interpretations, yet it clearly seems to envisage the possibility of a republican regime for Spain. Even under the existing system, Jovellanos favored, during the War of Independence, the institution of universal male franchise, though combined with limits on eligibility to office (I, 551a); and he proposed, though too late to save the Spanish empire, that the overseas colonies play an active part in the joint government (I, 602a).

Another of the hotly debated topics of the war years was freedom of the press, which we associate with democratic government. Jovellanos, in 1809, declared such freedom, by which he meant freedom from prior censorship, necessary for intellectual progress (I, 275b); but he also recognized its dangers in time of war and was displeased when it was proclaimed by the *cortes* in 1810 (I, 555b, 599b; IV, 471a). Before the war, Jovellanos had suggested that the performance of dramas, though not their publication, should be subject to the approval of the Royal Spanish Academy (I, 497b). He was irritated at the restrictions imposed by clerical censorship (D II, 149) and at the way in which it was exercised. Granting its necessity with respect to modern antireligious authors, he considered it absurd as a defense against Jews and Protestants, who no longer imperiled Spain's religious purity; and he found the censors of the Inquisition too ignorant and slow for the task, recommending instead that it be entrusted to the bishops (V, 333b-34a). This was in keeping with governmental policy, which sought to strengthen the authority of the bishops at the expense of the more independent Inquisition.

VII   *Utopianism*

Jovellanos is consistently antimilitaristic and links hell and

war as "the two most horrible things which can present themselves to the human spirit" (D I, 338). Alexander and Julius
Caesar, he writes, must be counted among "the greatest enemies
of the human race" (II, 132b). And even while elated by the
victory of allied arms over the French at Talavera, he reflects on
the hollowness of military triumphs: "Thus, while human blood
runs in rivers, the songs of victory and the hymns of gratitude
to heaven celebrate the miseries of poor mankind" (IV, 423a).

Jovellanos' repeatedly asserted belief in the possibility of human progress through education is perhaps most eloquently
expressed in the *Theoretical-Practical Treatise*, where we read:

Who cannot see that the very progress of education will some day lead,
first the enlightened nations of Europe and finally those of the entire
earth, to a general confederation whose aim will be to preserve for each
the enjoyment of the benefits it owes to heaven, to maintain among all an
inviolable and perpetual peace, and to restrain, not with armies nor with
cannon, but with the force of its voice, which will be stronger and more
terrible than they, any rash nation that may dare to disturb the calm and
happiness of the human race? Who, finally, cannot see that this confederation of the nations and societies that cover the earth is the only universal
society possible for the human race, the only one to which it seems called
by nature and religion, and the only one worthy of the high destinies
which the Creator marked for it? (I, 255a)

Man, according to Jovellanos, is indefinitely improvable, capa-
ble of a progress whose limits we do not and cannot know. This
is true of the individual and, by means of the conservation and
transmission of knowledge, of the species as well.[11]

Thus we find once more the unity of Jovellanos' thought. Political reform, moral betterment, economic development—all are
parts of that single arch whose keystone is education and over
which, when Jovellanos allowed himself to indulge in the utopian speculations so dear to his age, mankind was to pass into a
new and better world.

VIII   *Epitaph*

Jovellanos developed no consistent political theory. Dealing
almost always with urgent practical questions, he occasionally
contradicted himself; yet certain factors remained constant in
his thought. He clearly considered the welfare of the people as

the aim of political activity, whether under the old regime of Enlightened Despotism or in compromise with the formulas of the new liberal creed. Although he occasionally dreamed of a near-perfect world, he had little faith in revolutionary and utopian solutions to the problems of his time. History and law were for him the shapers of a people's political destiny. An aristocrat by birth and temperament, he called on his class to fulfill its obligations; and he came, in time of war, to an increased appreciation of the capacities of the people.

What was the impact of Jovellanos' political vision on the practical course of events? "The answer is sad indeed. Jovellanos' thought is crushed by the French invasion and by the antithesis which begins to take shape in the *cortes* of Cadiz, between the two schools [traditionalism and subversively revolutionary "philosophy"] which Jovellanos had condemned. Jovellanos' fate was that of all balanced and serene thought in those restless hours of history which always tend toward radical solutions."[12] In these words a distinguished contemporary Spanish historian has written the epitaph of Jovellanos' political thought. Yet that thought continues to be studied and to merit study as an example of Spain's Enlightenment and as part of a total vision of a society more just, more free, more prosperous, more educated—a society advancing in the pursuit of those two great eighteenth-century goals, virtue and material welfare.

CHAPTER 8

Miscellaneous Writings

I N other chapters of this study we have seen something of the amazing variety of Jovellanos' writings. Without trying to make a complete catalogue of all our author's works, we should now briefly examine a few additional topics to which he was led by his duties and his genuine breadth of interests, and two special genres which he cultivated with distinction.

I *Minor Topics*

Jovellanos, as a reformer, realized the importance of understanding the past, without which any attempt to improve the present is only arrogant ignorance. Thus his writings on the agrarian problem and on the State's policy toward public entertainments were preceded and supported by historical research. We have seen that the history of architecture also attracted Jovellanos. Furthermore, his diary shows him not only reading history, but also pursuing historical investigations on his travels. He was an indefatigable collector and copier of documents; and wherever his duties took him, he was sure to spend some time in the local archives. In its attention to documents, the historiography of the Enlightenment had progressed beyond purely humanistic historiography. It also began to study the history of commerce, industry, and other activities which before had seemed beneath the historian's notice, and to examine such matters from the point of view of the governed, not invariably that of the governors. In these respects Jovellanos, though not a professional historian, was abreast of the most advanced of his time. Indeed, in his emphasis on the importance of the unique national character as developed in the historical growth of institutions and laws, he anticipates the Romantic historians.[1] He knew that the texture of history is woven of many strands besides the will

of kings and the skill of generals, and he called for more attention to these ongoing historical processes and less insistence on
climactic and catastrophic events (I, 298). He consistently
stressed that the welfare of the governed is the aim of the
activities of government.

Don Gaspar also concerned himself with prison reform, believing that the evil influence of the most depraved convicts and
the equal treatment given to all prisoners were so depressing and
demoralizing as to make genuine rehabilitation almost a miracle.
He therefore urged that only those criminals who absolutely
could not be tolerated elsewhere should be imprisoned, while
the others should serve in the armed forces or on public works
projects, or be placed in "houses of correction." These were to
be a transitional stage between prison and liberty, with less hard
labor and more encouragement of habits of work and sobriety.
Former convicts, Jovellanos believed, should be obliged to
reside and work in their native towns, where their behavior
could be easily supervised by the local magistrates (I, 451 ff.).

Jovellanos devoted himself to the cultivation of the national
language, becoming a member of the Royal Spanish Academy
and leaving, among his papers, some notes toward the formation
of an etymological supplement to the Academy's dictionary
(Ceán, p. 212). More interesting, perhaps, is his concern with
Spain's local languages and dialects. He urged the study of
Majorcan Catalan, and he naturally paid special attention to the
dialect of Asturias. In a letter written in 1791, he expresses his
hope for its methodical investigation (IV, 170 ff.); and he later
joined some friends in planning the establishment of an Asturian
Academy, among whose tasks was to be the preparation of a dictionary complete with etymologies and documentation of usage,
for which proverbs, folk songs, and old poems were to be gathered and analyzed. About 1804, Jovellanos wrote his *Apunta-
mientos sobre el dialecto de Asturias* (*Notes on the Asturian
Dialect*), related to a planned geographical dictionary. In this
brief essay he stresses the importance of etymology for historical studies, explaining how the origin of a word can reveal the
origin and history of the object it signifies (I, 343-49).

Though Jovellanos' general vision of language seems modern,
some of his approaches and findings would not be accepted

today. The etymologies he proposes are sometimes capricious; and although he recognizes the value of non-Classical Latin as a source of the Romance languages, the relative importance he ascribes to it is the inverse of what a modern Romance linguist would teach: Jovellanos wants the etymon of every Asturian word to be sought in Classical Latin and only "if the root should not be discovered in good Latin, will it be sought in Low Latin, where many roots will be found" (II, 209a). When different pronunciations exist for a single word, Jovellanos prefers not the most common but that closest to the original Latin (II, 210a), a normative approach which no student of dialects would sustain today.

II   *Minor Genres*

Our author holds a distinguished place in the history of two genres but lightly represented in Spanish literature. To judge by surviving texts and the notes in his diary, Jovellanos was a tireless correspondent. His age valued the letter as a means of interpersonal contact and as a source of news; and it enjoyed such epistolary novels as Cadalso's *Moroccan Letters,* Montesquieu's *Persian Letters,* and Samuel Richardson's *Clarissa* and *Pamela.* Jovellanos' letters are not only examples of polished prose; they help us to understand their author's thought and to interpret the writings which he destined for publication. There is thus more than personal interest in reading Don Gaspar's extensive correspondence with Carlos González Posada or with Lord Holland, and every reason to lament the apparent loss or destruction of his letters to Alexander Jardine, the English radical.

Diaries and memoirs are also rare in Spanish literature. The preserved and published diary of Jovellanos covers, with many and occasionally sizeable lapses, nearly two decades of his life, from August 20, 1790, to March 6, 1810. Jovellanos probably also wrote a diary before and after these dates, but such texts are unknown to us.

The first edition of the diary carried the subtitle *Intimate Memoirs,* which, unfortunately for anyone seeking details, or even outlines, of Don Gaspar's amours, is quite misleading. Our author's sentimental life is forever hidden behind an impenetrable screen of modesty and decorum, which there is no point in trying to circumvent by means of fanciful conjectures. The diary offers us no confession, no self-analysis, and few witty or quasi-profound Great Thoughts about God, the Meaning of Life, etc. It does, however, reflect the broad range of Jovellanos' interests, both the important and the minute. In it we can follow the creation and operation of the Royal Asturian Institute; we can join Jovellanos on his travels and read his comments on roads and inns. We see his concern with cleanliness, with the quality of food and drink; his interest in amusements; his love of trees; his passion for antiquities, whether they be documents, buildings, or paintings; his close observation of local customs and the local economy. We find reflections of current events, great and small, together with Jovellanos' comments on them. And we can trace the development of Jovellanos' friendships, his correspondence, the course of his readings, his health, and even the weather. Some of the author's remarks are, in a sense, intimate, because they could not safely be divulged in his time; but others were intended for eventual publication, as Don Gaspar explains to González Posada: "How many things I've seen on my journey from Asturias to the French border! But they are in my diary; and some day you will see them, and perhaps the public, too, if God grants me leisure and tranquillity" (II, 172a).

Like Jovellanos' letters, his diary helps us to interpret those of his works published in his lifetime under an inhibiting censorship and to clarify the influences on his thought and writings. It also affords us a picture of the daily life of an educated gentleman in Enlightenment Spain, with an occasional quaint mixture of the petty and the important: "A bad night; the bed ill made; it turned into a precipice and I fought all night to escape it. How small are the things which cause our travails!" (D II, 19). "Home; reading in *The Life of Bacon*; pedicure; reading in Risco, Volume XXXIX" (D II, 22-23). Jovellanos' character as revealed in the diary does not differ substantially from what one would expect after reading his other works. Its outstanding traits are intellectual curiosity, loyalty to friends and country, devotion to the common good, an often poetic spirit, love of nature, and a straightforward religiosity unalloyed with affectation and bigotry. The absence of a certain kind of intimate confession reveals an unfailing dignity which may seem almost prudish to an age that no longer values privacy. Jovellanos' diary contrasts sharply with that of his younger contemporary, Leandro F. de Moratín. Moratín's pages are thoroughly intimate but quite unreadable; Jovellanos', in their more restrained way, are one of the most highly readable and, indeed, fascinating texts of his age.

CHAPTER 9

Summation

J OVELLANOS' writings did not exercise appreciable influence beyond the borders of the Spanish-speaking world. Very few were ever translated; and foreign readers generally have little knowledge of either the Spanish language or its literature, except for one or two figures of the first rank, to which our author did not belong. The significance of Jovellanos must therefore be sought entirely within the Hispanic realm. Here, as we have seen, his political thought had little immediate practical consequence, though Spain subsequently experimented with the constitutional monarchy and bicameral parliamentary system which he envisaged. On the other hand, his pedagogical theories, and his own implementation of them, influenced the educational reforms of the nineteenth century; and his works on economics contributed to the triumph of economic liberalism in Spain and Spanish America (Camacho, 289-93). We have seen that Jovellanos' writings on these subjects were in the main intended to deal with specific current problems and that, with the possible exception of the pedagogical writings (one of the most important of which, however, is unfinished), they are therefore not systematic expositions of doctrine. In fact, Jovellanos occasionally contradicts himself as he adjusts his thought to new circumstances.

In the domain of the more narrowly literary, Jovellanos' *The Honorable Culprit* showed the possibilities of serious realistic drama devoted to contemporary social issues, a genre which enjoyed a modest success until it was overpowered by the Romantic furor. As a poet, Jovellanos, besides writing a handful of masterpieces, helped, by teaching and example, to create around the turn of the century a more socially oriented poetry in the service of the ideals of the Enlightenment, as well as a poetry directly reflecting the sensations of daily life. Both in verse and in prose, he cultivated a flexible style, correct and elegant, yet open to innovation and thus a forerunner of the stylistic and linguistic freedom of Romanticism.

The variety of Jovellanos' works, both in subject and in genre —a variety which this study has by no means exhausted—testifies to the enormous range of our author's interests and curiosity. Within this variety, however, there is congruity of purpose: we find drama in the service of legal reform, economics designed to promote social justice and stressing the moral benefits of independent rural life, poetry criticizing social abuses and advocating political ideals, and descriptions of landscape in which usefulness to man is seen as the culminating beauty. Jovellanos, unwilling to consider life only as suffering, wished to further the material well-being of the individual, a respectable goal for those who are neither devotees of an otherwordly asceticism nor the pampered children of over-abundance. Even more, however, he sought the moral improvement of the individual, society, and the race. He had faith in reason, that imperfect, much-abused, much-maligned, but still unique and indispensable instrument; and he believed that education, which he saw as the perfection of reason (I, 232b), would allow man to progress to limits as yet indiscernible.

Utility and truth, the aims which Jovellanos set for the Royal Asturian Institute, were also his own goals, together with virtue. "Life is short," he wrote a friend, "and to fill its term usefully we must hurry. After devoting to that everlasting [life] which awaits us the time and attention which it deserves more than anything else, what better employment shall we find for these sad and fleeting moments than to increase the small supply of truth, whatever its purpose? Or, at least, what use more innocent and sweet?" (II, 214a). Idle speculation, however, did not attract Jovellanos. The truths he most valued were those which would better mankind and its lot on earth.

From Jovellanos' writings there emerges the figure of a man who was pious without superstition, patriotic without chauvinism, loyal in friendship, compassionate of the sufferings of his fellowmen, seeking always to serve others, never himself. He believed that we are social beings; and he held high standards of a citizen's duty, with which his talents and inclinations coincided to an unusually felicitous degree. Ultimately, this figure of a man whose life was dedicated to truth, utility, and virtue is Jovellanos' greatest work. For those who come to know it, its nobility is undeniable, and its attraction, irresistible. I hope that this book may have done something to reveal it to the reader.

Notes and References

Chapter One

1. The main historical sources used in this chapter are Antonio Ferrer del Río, *Historia del reinado de Carlos III en España,* 4 vols. (Madrid, 1856), Richard Herr, *The Eighteenth-Century Revolution in Spain* (Princeton, 1958), and Modesto Lafuente, *Historia general de España desde los tiempos primitivos hasta la muerte de Fernando VII*, XV-XVII (Barcelona, 1889). The main biographical source on Jovellanos is Juan Agustín Ceán Bermúdez, *Memorias para la vida del Excmo. Señor D. Gaspar Melchor de Jove Llanos, y noticias analíticas de sus obras* (Madrid, 1814 [1820]), hereafter cited as Ceán.

2. José Caso González, ed., *Poesías,* by Jovellanos (Oviedo, 1961), pp. 19-22. This work is hereafter cited as Caso, *Poesías.*

3. José Caso González, "Jovellanos y la Inquisición (un intento inquisitorial de prohibir el 'Informe sobre Ley Agraria' en 1797)," *Archivum*, VII (1957), 257; José Caso González, "Rectificaciones y apostillas a mi artículo 'Jovellanos y la Inquisición,'" *Archivum*, IX (1959), 93; Lafuente, XV, 345.

4. Julio Somoza, García-Sala, *Documentos para escribir la biografía de Jovellanos* (Madrid, 1911), I, 225 ff.

5. Edith F. Helman, "Some Consequences of the Publication of the *Informe de Ley Agraria* by Jovellanos," in *Estudios hispánicos: homenaje a Archer M. Huntington* (Wellesley, Mass., 1952), p. 272, n. 46.

6. *Noticias históricas de D. Gaspar Melchor de Jovellanos* (Palma, 1812), p. 48.

Chapter Two

1. Caso, *Poesías*, p. 109. This edition is used for all references to and quotations from Jovellanos' poetry.

2. *Ibid.*, p. 70. My colleague, Professor Luis Monguió, found the "Asturian Battle Hymn," without indication of author, in

the *Gazeta del Gobierno de Lima*, No. 24 (Lima, February 1, 1811), Suplemento.

3. *Poetas líricos del siglo XVIII*, ed. Leopoldo Augusto de Cueto (Madrid, 1869-1875), II (Biblioteca de Autores Españoles, LXIII), 112.

4. Joaquín Arce, "Jovellanos y la sensibilidad prerromántica," *Boletín de la Biblioteca de Menéndez Pelayo*, XXXVI (1960), 155-56; Caso, *Poesías*, pp. 34-36 and notes on pp. 447-53.

5. *Poetas líricos del siglo XVIII*, II, 73 ff.

6. See note 4.

7. José Caso González and Georges Demerson, "La sátira de Jovellanos sobre la mala educación de la nobleza (versión original, corregida por Meléndez Valdés)," *Bulletin Hispanique*, LXI (1959), 367; Caso, *Poesías*, p. 241.

8. Caso, *Poesías*, pp. 40 ff., 423, and my review of this edition, *Hispanic Review*, XXXVI (1968), 179. The text of the letters, in *ed. cit.*, pp. 423-33.

9. My student John Petrovsky investigated some of these in a paper in 1967.

10. " 'Entretenimientos juveniles de Jovino': Un manuscrito de Menéndez Pelayo y una versión inédita de la 'Epístola del Paular,' " *Boletín de la Biblioteca de Menéndez Pelayo*, XXXVI (1960), 109-38.

11. *Tomás Navarro, Métrica española: reseña histórica y descriptiva* (Syracuse, 1956), p. 312; Enrique de Gandía, "Las ideas políticas de Jovellanos," *La nueva democracia*, XXXIX, No. 3 (July, 1959), 41.

12. See José María Martínez Cachero, "Jovellanos ante la poesía," in Real Instituto "Jovellanos" de Enseñanza Media, *Memoria del curso 1961-1962* (Gijón, 1963), pp. 78-90; Arce, pp. 140 ff.; Caso, *Poesías*, pp. 9, 36.

Chapter Three

1. Ada M. Coe, *Catálogo bibliográfico y crítico de las comedias anunciadas en los periódicos de Madrid desde 1661 hasta 1819* (Baltimore, 1935), lists *La [sic] Munuza* for that year.

2. Emilio Cotarelo y Mori, *Iriarte y su época* (Madrid, 1897), p. 69.

3. The date usually given is 1738; but see José Caso González, "El Delincuente honrado, drama sentimental," *Archi-*

vum, XIV (1964), 109.

4. Paul Geneste, study cited as unpublished by José Caso González, "Notas críticas de bibliografía jovellanista (1950-1959)," *Boletín de la Biblioteca de Menéndez Pelayo*, XXXVI (1960), 212.

5. Ángel Ossorio y Gallardo, "Jovellanos jurista," in *Jovellanos: su vida y su obra: homenaje del Centro Asturiano de Buenos Aires en el bicentenario de su nacimiento, con la adhesión de los Centros Asturianos de la Habana y México* (Buenos Aires, 1945), pp. 152 ff.

6. Caso, "El Delincuente honrado," p. 125.

7. John H. R. Polt, "Jovellanos' *El delincuente honrado*," *The Romanic Review*, L (1959), 173.

8. Thomas Hobbes, *Leviathan*, Chapter XXVII; Charles de Secondat, Baron de Montesquieu, *De l'Esprit des lois*, Book III, Chapter VII, and Book IV, Chapter II; Cesare Beccaria, *Dei delitti e delle pene*, Chapter XXIX.

9. Denis Diderot, *Entretiens sur le Fils naturel, Œuvres complètes*, ed. J. Assézat, VII (Paris, 1875), 150.

10. *De la Poésie dramatique, Œuvres complètes*, VII, 311-12.

11. Concerning this last feature, see Arce, p. 161, n. 48.

12. Cf. comments on the First Satire, p. 43 above. For sources of *The Honorable Culprit*, see the articles by Caso, Polt, and Jean Sarrailh, "À propos du *Delincuente honrado* de Jovellanos," in *Mélanges d'études portugaises offerts à M. Georges Le Gentil* ([Chartres]: Instituto para a Alta Cultura, 1949), pp. 337-51.

13. Antonio Alcalá Galiano, *Historia de la literatura española, francesa, inglesa e italiana en el siglo XVIII* (Madrid, 1845), p. 378.

14. Ramón del Toro y Durán, *Jovellanos y la reforma del teatro español en el siglo XVIII* (Gijón, 1891), p. 66; *El intérprete del pueblo*, No. 16 (Lima, Feb. 11, 1852), a reference which I owe to the generosity of D. Luis Monguió.

15. Russell P. Sebold, "Contra los mitos antineoclásicos españoles," *Papeles de Son Armadans*, IX, No. CIII (October, 1964), pp. 108-10.

16. Julio Somoza de Montsoriú, *Inventario de un jovellanista* (Madrid, 1901), p. 126.

17. Fermín Canella y Secades, *Historia de la Universidad de Oviedo y noticias de los establecimientos de enseñanza de su distrito*, 2d ed. (Oviedo, 1903), p. 352, n. 1.

Chapter Four

1. See V, 377 ff., and Paul Ilie, "Picturesque Beauty in Spain and England: Aesthetic Rapports between Jovellanos and Gilpin," *The Journal of Aesthetics and Art Criticism,* XIX (1960-1961), 167-74.

2. On Jovellanos and Goya, see Edith F. Helman, *Trasmundo de Goya* (Madrid, 1963).

3. I, 360a, 375a. See also Ilie, p. 167, and Ricardo del Arco, "Jovellanos y las bellas artes," *Revista de ideas estéticas,* IV (1946), 42-43.

4. For bringing these paintings to my attention I am grateful to Miss Áurea de la Morena Bartolomé of the University of Madrid.

5. Jovellanos, *Reglamento para el Colegio de Calatrava,* ed. José Caso González (Gijón, 1964), p. 136. This work is hereafter cited as *Calatrava.*

6. Ed. of *Visiones y visitas de Torres con don Francisco de Quevedo por la corte,* by Diego de Torres Villarroel (Madrid; Clásicos Castellanos, 1966), pp. lvii ff.

Chapter Five

1. Borrego, *Der Nationalreichtum, die Finanzen und die Staatsschuld des Königreichs Spanien* (Mannheim, 1834), cited in Rudolf Leonhard, *Agrarpolitik und Agrarreform in Spanien unter Carl III* (Munich and Berlin, 1909), p. 46, n. 2; Vicente Palacio Atard, *Fin de la sociedad española del antiguo régimen* (Madrid, 1952), pp. 10-15.

2. See Earl J. Hamilton, *War and Prices in Spain, 1651-1800* (Cambridge, Mass., 1947).

3. A brief abstract of these, with comments by Jovellanos, is preserved in the Public Library of Gijón, Manuscripts of Jovellanos, Carpeta No. 2.

4. II, 149. See my *Jovellanos and his English Sources: Economic, Philosophical, and Political Writings.* Transactions of the American Philosophical Society, New Series, Vol. 54, Part 7 (Philadelphia, 1964), pp. 39-40.

5. See Caso, "Jovellanos y la Inquisición" and "Rectificaciones y apostillas"; Helman, "Some Consequences"; and Herr, p. 397.

6. II, 103b; cf. Francis Hutcheson, *A System of Moral Phi-*

losophy (Glasgow, 1755), pp. 309 ff. Concerning Jovellanos and Hutcheson, see *Calatrava*, p. 175.

7. II, 36a, 82a; Adam Smith, *An Inquiry into the Nature and Causes of the Wealth of Nations*, ed. Edwin Cannan (New York, 1937), pp. 121-22.

8. See my *Jovellanos and his English Sources*, pp. 34-36.

9. *Ibid.*, pp. 20-21.

10. Public Library of Gijón, Manuscripts of Jovellanos, Carpeta No. 3, Item No. 58, Letter 7 (1796-1797). Cf. I, 231a.

11. See Osvaldo Chiareno, "Jovellanos economista e la lingua del suo 'Informe sobre la Ley Agraria,'" *Bollettino dell' Istituto di Lingue Estere*, No. 3 (1952-1953), 46-60.

Chapter Six

1. See Jean Sarrailh, *L'Espagne éclairée de la seconde moitié du XVIIIe siècle* (Paris, 1954), Part II, Chapter I: "La Croyance en la culture."

2. On Spanish education in the eighteenth century, see, in addition to Sarrailh and others, G. Desdevises du Dézert, *L'Espagne de l'ancien régime*, 3 vols. (Paris, 1897-1904), and John Raymond Perz, *Secondary Education in Spain* (Washington, 1934).

3. D I, 454 refers to the "Plan" of I, 101-4. See Somoza, *Inventario*, p. 154; Caso, *Poesías*, p. 17, n. 1; Gabriel Llabrés, "Jovellanos en Mallorca (1801-1808)," *Boletín de la Sociedad Arqueológica Luliana*, VII (1891), 117.

4. Somoza, *Inventario*, p. 82; Caso, "Notas críticas," p. 187.

5. On Jovellanos and scholasticism, see Juan Luis Villota Elejalde, *Doctrinas filosófico-jurídicas y morales de Jovellanos* (Oviedo, 1958), and José Caso González, "Escolásticos e innovadores a finales del siglo XVIII (Sobre el catolicismo de Jovellanos)," *Papeles de Son Armadans*, No. CIX (April, 1965), pp. 25-48.

6. IV, 232b. Charles Bonnet was a Genevese philosopher of the eighteenth century. Antonio Eximeno (1729-1808), a priest, takes a Lockeian approach within a scholastic style, presumably purging the doctrines of Locke and Condillac of theologically objectionable notions. I believe this to be the meaning of Jovellanos' comment on him.

7. Public Library of Gijón, Manuscripts of Jovellanos, Carpeta No. 3, Item No. 58, Letter 3 (1796-1797).

8. V, 16b; cf. I, 240a. Jovellanos' authorship of the first-cited item has been questioned but, in my opinion, successfully vindicated by Harold Lowe Dowdle, "The Humanitarianism of Gaspar Melchor de Jovellanos," unpublished dissertation (Stanford, 1954), pp. 238 ff.

9. See my *Jovellanos and his English Sources*, pp. 46-48.

10. Antonio de Capmany, *Arte de traducir el idioma francés al castellano* (Madrid, 1776), Prologue, quoted in [Cipriano Muñoz y Manzano,] conde de la Viñaza, *Biblioteca histórica de la filología castellana* (Madrid, 1893), p. 906.

11. Caso, "Escolásticos e innovadores."

12. Georges Demerson, "Un canarien 'éclairé': D. Estanislao de Lugo (1753-1833)," in *Mélanges à la mémoire de Jean Sarrailh* (Paris, 1966), pp. 316-17.

13. María Ángeles Galino Carrillo, *Tres hombres y un problema: Feijóo, Sarmiento y Jovellanos ante la educación moderna* (Madrid, 1953), p. 241.

14. Ángel María Camacho y Perea, *Estudio crítico de las doctrinas de Jovellanos en lo referente a las ciencias morales y políticas* (Madrid, 1913), pp. 259-60.

Chapter Seven

1. Polt, *Jovellanos and his English Sources*, pp. 9-10, 53-57.

2. Adam Ferguson, *Institutes of Moral Philosophy for the Use of Students in the College of Edinburgh,* 2d ed. (Edinburgh, 1773), pp. 199-205, and *An Essay on the History of Civil Society* (Edinburgh, 1767), pp. 3-9.

3. Luis Sánchez Agesta, *El pensamiento político del despotismo ilustrado* (Madrid, 1953), pp. 94-95.

4. "Of the True Greatnesse of Kingdomes and Estates," *Essays*, ed. Wright, pp. 119-22, quoted by Eli F. Heckscher, *Mercantilism*, ed. E. F. Söderlund, rev. [2d] ed., trans. Mendel Shapiro (London, 1955), II, 45.

5. *Rights of Man: Being an Answer to Mr. Burke's Attack on the French Revolution*, Part I (London, 1792), p. 29.

6. *Reflections on the Revolution in France, and on the Proceedings in Certain Societies in London Relative to that Event*, 4th ed. (London, 1790), pp. 50 ff.

7. Public Library of Gijón, Manuscripts of Jovellanos, Carpeta No. 3, Item No. 21.

8. See my *Jovellanos and his English Sources*, p. 65.

9. *Two Treatises of Government*, ed. Peter Laslett (Cambridge, England, 1960), pp. 384-85.

10. D I, 432, 436-37; II, 366-67. Concerning the latter text see my "Una nota jovellanista: Carta *A desconocida persona*," in *Homenaje a Rodríguez-Moñino: Estudios de erudición que le ofrecen sus amigos o discípulos hispanistas norteamericanos* (Madrid, 1966), II, 81-86.

11. Public Library of Gijón, Manuscripts of Jovellanos. Carpeta No. 3, Item No. 58, Letters 5 and 6.

12. Luis Sánchez Agesta, "España y Europa en el pensamiento español del siglo XVIII," *Cuadernos de la Cátedra Feijóo*, No. 2 (Oviedo, 1955), p. 27.

Chapter Eight

1. Claudio Sánchez Albornoz, "Jovellanos y la historia," in *Jovellanos: su vida y su obra* (see above, Chapter 3, n. 5), pp. 561 ff., 588-90 (reprinted in his *Españoles ante la historia* [Buenos Aires, 1958], pp. 176 ff., 206).

Selected Bibliography

PRIMARY SOURCES

Works by Gaspar Melchor de Jovellanos

Colección de varias obras en prosa y verso, ed. Ramón María Cañedo. 7 vols. Madrid: Imprenta de D. León Amarita, 1830-1832. This first collection of Jovellanos' works is neither complete nor very reliable.

Obras publicadas e inéditas. 5 vols.: I and II, ed. Cándido Nocedal. Madrid: Rivadeneyra (Biblioteca de Autores Españoles, XLVI and L), 1858-1859. III-V, ed. Miguel Artola, Madrid: Ediciones Atlas (Biblioteca de Autores Españoles, LXXXV-LXXXVII), 1956. The most extensive and accessible collection, but almost unannotated and deficiently edited.

Obras escogidas, ed. Ángel del Río. 3 vols. Madrid: Espasa-Calpe (Clásicos Castellanos), 1935-1946. An easily available selection of prose, with an introduction by a distinguished Hispanist.

Diarios, ed. Julio Somoza, with a preliminary study by Ángel del Río and indices by José María Martínez Cachero. 3 vols. Oviedo: Instituto de Estudios Asturianos, 1953-1955. The best edition of Jovellanos' diary.

Poesías, ed. José Caso González. Oviedo: Instituto de Estudios Asturianos, 1961. Carefully edited and thoroughly annotated texts of Jovellanos' poetry.

Reglamento para el Colegio de Calatrava, ed. José Caso González. Gijón: Editorial Stella, 1964. The best edition of one of Jovellanos' pedagogical writings.

Espectáculos y diversiones públicas. El castillo de Bellver. Madrid: Espasa-Calpe (Colección Austral), 1966. An easily available edition of two interesting works.

Diarios, ed. Julián Marías. Madrid: Alianza Editorial, 1967. A brief and easily available selection from Jovellanos' diary.

Obras en prosa, ed. José Caso González. Madrid: Castalia, 1969. An easily available, fairly extensive selection with notes and biographical and critical introduction.

SECONDARY SOURCES

1. Bibliographies

Somoza de Montsoriú, Julio. *Inventario de un jovellanista, con variada y copiosa noticia de impresos y manuscritos, publicaciones periódicas, traducciones, dedicatorias, epigrafía, grabado, escultura, etc., etc.* Madrid: Sucesores de Rivadeneyra, 1901. A bibliography of works by and about Jovellanos up to 1901, with miscellaneous additional information.

Suárez, Constantino. *Escritores y artistas asturianos: índice biobibliográfico,* IV, 532-616. Oviedo: Instituto de Estudios Asturianos, 1955. A biography of Jovellanos is followed by bibliography for 1902-1950, prepared by José María Martínez Cachero.

Caso González, José. "Notas críticas de bibliografía jovellanista (1950-1959)," *Boletín de la Biblioteca de Menéndez Pelayo,* XXXVI (1960), 179-213. The latest bibliography.

2. Other Studies

Arce, Joaquín. "Jovellanos y la sensibilidad prerromántica," *Boletín de la Biblioteca de Menéndez Pelayo,* XXXVI (1960), 139-77. This article analyzes Pre-Romantic tendencies in Jovellanos' poetry and the relations between Jovellanos and other poets of his time.

Arco, Ricardo del. "Jovellanos y las bellas artes," *Revista de ideas estéticas,* IV (1946), 31-64. Jovellanos' opinions on the arts of painting, sculpture, and architecture are compared to those current in his time.

Artíñano y de Galdácano, Gervasio de. *Jovellanos y su España,* Madrid, 1913. Interesting information on the Spain of the eighteenth century and good résumés of Jovellanos' thought.

Camacho y Perea, Ángel María. *Estudio crítico de las doctrinas de Jovellanos en lo referente a las ciencias morales y políti-*

cas. Madrid, 1913. A study of Jovellanos' political thought and related writings.

Caso González, José. "El delincuente honrado, drama sentimental," *Archivum*, XIV (1964), 103-33. The latest study on Jovellanos' prose drama.

—————. "Escolásticos e innovadores a finales del siglo XVIII (Sobre el catolicismo de Jovellanos)," *Papeles de Son Armadans*, No. CIX (April, 1965), 25-48. This article examines and refutes the accusations of heterodoxy brought against Jovellanos.

—————. *Jovellanos y la reforma de la enseñanza.* This book, still in press, promises to study one of the most important aspects of Jovellanos' work.

Ceán Bermúdez, Juan Agustín. *Memorias para la vida del Excmo. Señor D. Gaspar Melchor de Jove Llanos, y noticias analíticas de sus obras.* Madrid: Imprenta que fue de Fuentenebro, 1814 [1820]. The basic biography of Jovellanos, written by his lifelong friend.

Galino Carrillo, María Ángeles. *Tres hombres y un problema: Feijoo, Sarmiento y Jovellanos ante la educación moderna.* Madrid: Consejo Superior de Investigaciones Científicas, 1953. Educational reform in the writings of three outstanding Spaniards of the Enlightenment.

Jovellanos: su vida y su obra. Homenaje del Centro Asturiano de Buenos Aires en el bicentenario de su nacimiento, con la adhesión de los Centros Asturianos de la Habana y México. Buenos Aires, 1945. A collection of articles, of widely different merit, on various aspects of Jovellanos' life and works.

Polt, John H. R. "Jovellanos' *El delincuente honrado,*" *The Romanic Review*, L (1959), 170-90. This article studies the genesis, structure, and sources of Jovellanos' play.

—————. *Jovellanos and his English Sources: Economic, Philosophical, and Political Writings.* Transactions of the American Philosophical Society, New Series, Vol. 54, Part 7. Philadelphia: The American Philosophical Society, 1964.

—————. "Jovellanos y la educación," in *El P. Feijoo y su siglo: Ponencias y comunicaciones presentadas al simposio celebrado en la Universidad de Oviedo del 28 de septiembre al 5 de octubre de 1964. Cuadernos de la Cátedra Feijoo*, No. 18 (Oviedo, 1966), pp. 315-38. A study of Jovellanos' pedagogical theories and their implementation.

Prados Arrarte, Jesús. *Jovellanos, economista.* Madrid: Taurus,

1967. This comprehensive study first appeared in *Jovellanos: su vida y su obra.*

Ricard, Robert. "Jovellanos y la nobleza," *Atlántida*, III (1965), 456-72. Analysis of Jovellanos' ideas on the function and state of hereditary nobility.

Sánchez Agesta, Luis. *El pensamiento político del despotismo ilustrado.* Madrid: Instituto de Estudios Políticos, 1953. Part III of this important study deals with the political thought of Jovellanos.

Sarrailh, Jean. "À propos du *Delincuente honrado* de Jovellanos," in *Mélanges d'études portugaises offerts à M. Georges Le Gentil*, pp. 337-51. [Chartres]: Instituto para a Alta Cultura, 1949. The literary and legal background of Jovellanos' play.

————. *L'Espagne éclairée de la seconde moitié du XVIIIe siècle*, Paris: Imprimerie Nationale, 1954. Translated by Antonio Alatorre as *La España ilustrada de la segunda mitad del siglo XVIII.* Mexico and Buenos Aires: Fondo de Cultura Económica, 1957. Jovellanos plays a major role in this fundamental study of the Spanish Enlightenment.

Somoza García-Sala, Julio [the same as Somoza de Montsoriú]. *Documentos para escribir la biografía de Jovellanos.* 2 vols. Madrid, 1911. Contains many interesting documents of a biographical nature, some of which have been subsequently reprinted in Jovellanos' *Obras publicadas e inéditas.*

Villota Elejalde, Juan Luis. *Doctrinas filosófico-jurídicas y morales de Jovellanos.* Oviedo: Instituto de Estudios Asturianos, 1958. This book seeks to show Jovellanos' debt to scholasticism.

Index